Beside the sea

Beside the sea

Tony and Hilary Soper

Illustrated by Maggie Raynor

BRITISH BROADCASTING CORPORATION

This book is published in conjunction
with the BBC television series *Beside the Sea*,
first transmitted on BBC-2 from Thursday 24 May 1979
The book is edited by Ron Bloomfield and the
series is produced by Ron Bloomfield and Judy Brooks

For Tim

Published to accompany a series of programmes
prepared in consultation with the
BBC Further Education Advisory Council

© Tony and Hilary Soper 1979
First published 1979
Published by the British Broadcasting Corporation
35 Marylebone High Street, London W1M 4AA

Printed in England by Balding and Mansell
Set in 11/12½ pt Monophoto Photina
ISBN 0 563 16285 6

Contents

Introduction

Most of us have a special affection for the environment in which we spent our first years. Whether it was town or suburb, hill farm or village green, the memory is powerfully evocative. Yet wherever we spent those years, most of us have equally powerful memories of visits to the seaside, for the coast has a magnetic attraction all of its own.

The seaside belongs to us all. Or at least, we like to think it does. In fact, well over a quarter of the 2750 miles of coastline in England and Wales is already built up in one way or another. Less than a quarter of it is 'protected' by nature reserves and the like, and almost all of it belongs to the Crown.

Of course, the coast has a very long history of settlement, but it is only relatively recently that people have regarded it as a place of pilgrimage and pleasure. Until the seventeenth century the fishermen had it pretty much to themselves. The first to discover its pleasure potential were those who journeyed to the coastal spas to indulge in sea bathing for the good of their health, only to discover that they enjoyed the convivial company and the splash of the waves.

Coastal resorts catered first for the gentry, then, with the arrival of the railway, for the trippering masses. Soon the visitors discovered the joys of the rock pool, and entered with gusto into the age of 'collecting'. The sea-plants and sea-creatures fascinated the Victorians, as they fascinate anyone who casts so much as a first careless glance in their direction.

The people who started to use the coast as a 'resort' became very much aware of the charm of the place. Unlike the fishermen, whose cottages turned their backs to the sea and

'Common objects at the seaside – generally found upon the rocks at low water.' *Punch*, 1858.

who cursed when gales kept them ashore with empty bellies, the newcomers built houses with bay windows and balconies facing the sea, so that they could enjoy and marvel at its moods. For one of the great appeals of the seaside is its quality of constant change. Watching a sharp horizon blur as a squall approaches, sweeping brighter skies in its wake, is unmatched by any change of mood ashore. Seeing a calm blue sea turn slate grey and sprout white horses on its mounting waves is to gain a true insight into the power of old 'earth shaker'.

The changes in colour and movement of the sea are all gloriously unpredictable, depending on the weather, but one kind of change can be predicted fairly accurately, and that is the tide. The rhythm of the tide must form the framework for any holiday exploration of the seaside, and a rough understanding of its nature is essential for real enjoyment of shore-going. You will need to look at the tidal information in the local paper, or glean it from the radio, but best of all buy a copy of the tide tables for your chosen port. For every day of the year your tide table will list the times of high water and the times of low water, and the heights to which these tides will rise. Weather conditions may modify the figures (very low pressure, for example, will prevent the tide from rising to its allotted height), but it is possible to pinpoint these times and levels because they are under the control of a very predictable body – the moon.

The earth and the moon have a gravitational attraction for each other, and the force is exerted in a straight line between the two bodies. The nearer a place is to the moon, the stronger will be the pull of gravity. When gravity acts on the great mass of water in the oceans, it has the effect of 'sucking it up' in the direction of the gravitational pull. The effect of this 'sucking up' of the water is to produce higher tides in areas of the earth closest to the moon, and consequently lower tides on the other side of the world. Because the moon is rotating in an orbit round the earth, the places experiencing high and low tides at any particular time are constantly changing in cyclic fashion.

Most places in Britain have two high and two low water periods every twenty-four hours. Between these peaks and troughs the water rises for approximately six hours from low water to high water (flooding) and falls for the same period when the tide is said to be 'ebbing', until it reaches low water. The difference in height between these two levels is known as the 'range' of the tide. As the tide rises and falls, water is being moved from one part of the coast to another creating a 'tidal current', which is the result of the difference in height between the two places. In the English Channel, for example, the current during flood tide is always from west to east, since the time of high water is progressively later as you travel eastwards. These currents may sometimes be very powerful, forming rips and tide-races, depending on the configuration of the coastline, and where they impinge on the beach itself they will affect the plants and animals that live there.

Another important aspect of the change between high and low water is the uneven rate of the rise and fall during the passage of the tide. When the tide is flooding, the first third of the rise takes two hours, the second third takes only one hour, while the last third takes three hours to rise. When the tide is ebbing the situation is reversed and it takes three hours to fall

the first third, again one hour for the second third and two hours for the third. So in the middle of the range, whether the tide is ebbing or flooding, the speed of change is at its greatest. This is valuable information, allowing you to work out how much time you have to explore the low water ledges, and when to leave your private bay to avoid being cut off by the tide.

How high the tide will rise and how low it will fall depend upon the phases of the moon. At new and full moon, when the earth, the moon and the sun lie in a straight line and the effect of gravity is at its greatest, the tides, known as 'springs', will have their greatest range, producing the highest high tides and the lowest low tides. For the seven days following each new or full moon, the three heavenly bodies gradually move out of alignment until the sun and the moon lie at right-angles to the earth, when the effect of gravity is least. Now the tides are known as 'neaps', and they rise less and fall the least. Between neaps and springs the range gradually builds up and then down again every seven days, thus 'making' and 'taking off'. As the tides build towards springs, each successive strandline will be removed, so that the receding water leaves just one strand of debris across the beach. As they take off, especially if conditions are calm and stable, the debris of each successive tide will remain, leaving several strandlines of tide-borne debris for the diligent beachcomber to explore.

Twice a year, at the spring and autumn equinox, when in response to the rhythm of the sun's annual orbit of the earth, the earth, moon and sun achieve their most perfect linear alignment, the equinoctial spring tides occur, and the coast suffers its greatest tidal inundation as well as its lowest tides. These equinoctial springs occur about 21st March and 21st September each year, and the excitement comes at the low water period when plants, animals, submerged seaweed forests or ancient wrecks which normally lie below the surface are exposed to the air and open for inspection. Whether these low water bonanzas occur at night or during daylit hours depends on what part of the country you are in, but darkness need be no deterrent. A torch-lit expedition to the lowest parts of the shore has its own excitement, very different to the day.

An understanding of tidal phenomena and a quick look at the ordnance survey map are all you need to start on an exploration of the most varied and rewarding of all habitats, the coast. So without more ado, let us take off our shoes and socks, and get the feel of the sand and sea water between our toes!

The living sea

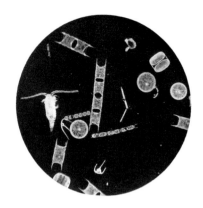

At first sight the sea appears no more than a great expanse of water. Cup your hands for a sample and the result looks as clear as tap water, but there is a different feel to it, and most certainly a different taste. Take a couple of gallons and boil it dry over a beach fire, and you will produce the best part of a cupful of excellent, if rather smoky, sea-salt. The off-white crystalline rime that you scrape from the pan will be mostly sodium chloride, but there will be small quantities of other chemicals and traces of almost any mineral you care to mention.

The nutrient salts, in solution, maintain a huge quantity of plant growth. Whereas on land our familiar plants derive their nutriment from the soil, in the open sea the plants drift in rootless fashion and absorb the phosphates and nitrates which surround them. Tiny and almost invisible to the naked eye, they co-exist in vast quantities with microscopic animals, always near the surface, where they can take advantage of the sunlight to build up sugar supplies, using the carbon dioxide breathed out by the animals which, in turn, live off the plant pasture and benefit from the oxygen it produces.

Together, these plants and animals are known as *plankton*, and their characteristic is that they inhabit the surface regions and drift freely at the mercy of the current. Both plant and animal members of the plankton have some power of movement, though, for without it they would inevitably sink, and in sinking out of reach of sunlight they would die. Some have the capacity to vary the proportions of water and fats in their bodies, using the buoyancy of oil to float themselves up to the surface. Some have long spines or feather-like processes which reduce the rate at which they sink by increasing frictional resistance. And some of the animals can actively propel themselves upward. Some of the jellyfishes, for example, the largest and most visible of the plankton animals, can jet-propel themselves through the water using muscular force, while others stay at the surface by providing themselves with floats in the shape of bladders, like the Portuguese man-o'-war.

The surface-drifting plant community is known as *phytoplankton* and their animal counterpart as *zooplankton*. And these two divisions, each dependent on the other and nourished by gases and salts, are the vital foundation stones for higher life in the sea.

To gain some idea of the teeming life in the surface layer of the sea, we towed a cone-shaped net made of fine nylon for just a few minutes in the waters of Plymouth Sound. Hauled back on board, the interior of the net was coated with a layer of sludge. Carefully scraped off and transferred to a jar of seawater, it was immediately clear that the 'sludge' was full of life. Little creatures jumped and darted about in the water. When a drop of it was put under the microscope, the varied shapes were fascinating. Most of the specimens were transparent, but nevertheless full of interest. The plant life was represented by the single-celled diatoms and dinoflagellates, waving their tiny whiplashes in the constant task of maintaining depth. The animals were larval forms of fish, crustaceans and molluscs. Many easily recognisable barnacle larvae were there.

Most of the animals of the sea, whether they are worms, starfishes, crabs, snails, or fishes, start their lives as larvae, drifting with and feeding on the plant pasture. A very large percentage of them end their lives there as well, eaten by something larger; but one of the great advantages of this way of life is that it ensures dispersal at the juvenile stage of creatures which in their adult form will be of a sedentary nature, perhaps even to the extent of being physically attached to a permanent home site.

The fact that a very large percentage of the plankton is eaten by something larger is no accident: it is part of the fundamental economy of the sea. An animal larva may eat some of the phytoplankton, only to be eaten itself by a small fish. The fish then forms part of a mackerel's breakfast, and the mackerel is eaten for dinner by a shark, and thus we have a classic 'food chain'. At the top of each food chain comes the biggest predator, say a killer whale, but in due course he too will die and his decaying remains form food for the plankton and the cycle is revitalised.

Sometimes the phytoplankton growth may be so prolific that it imparts a definite colour to the sea, perhaps red or yellow. These plankton blooms, for instance 'red tides', may have a disastrous effect because their potentially poisonous mineral contents may be concentrated in the animals which eat too much of them. This in turn may cause subsequent distress, or even death, to animals higher up the food chain. Thus seabirds which have eaten molluscs containing high concentrations of toxic dinoflagellates have been found dead on the shore. People who have eaten cockles or mussels affected by the 'red tide' may suffer serious, or even fatal, attacks of bellyache. The molluscs are apparently unaffected, simply acting as agents for poisons which they pass on to predators.

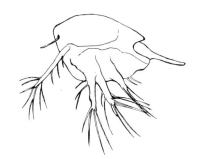

Nauplius larva of the acorn barnacle, *Balanus balanoides* (enlarged). After its drifting period in the plankton, the larva attaches itself to a hard surface, develops protective plates and uses its legs to scoop food particles from the passing current.

The pastures of the sea have their seasons in much the same way as those of the land, though their progression is not seen so clearly by us sea-watchers. The major influences, as on land, are the changes in day-length and temperature associated with the solar cycle. In spring the plants multiply and thrive on the extra light, then in summer, triggered by the warmth, the animals release their spawn to feed on the rich pasture, so that in summer the zooplankton is in the ascendant. When the autumn gales stir up the sea-bed and bring a flush of fresh nutrient-rich debris to the surface the phytoplankton enjoys a brief extra period of flowering. Then in winter the period of plenty is over and, as on land, the sea animals face the time of test, only the fittest passing the selection board and surviving to continue their life-cycle. Nevertheless the sea seasons are not so marked as those ashore, and one of the great advantages of a marine existence is that it offers a reasonably stable environment, where temperature change, for instance, is slow. While the hottest days on land may be in June, it is August/September before the sea achieves its greatest warmth. No wild daily fluctuations here.

The plankton plants and animals are at the mercy of tidal currents, but the two other great divisions of life at sea have a certain independence. The *nekton* comprises all those animals which have the facility of swimming, and the *benthos* includes those animals which make a living on the sea bed, taking advantage of the rain of organic debris that drifts down from the surface regions. Both divisions include animals from different classes, but in each case fish are the most highly and successfully adapted to the aquatic life. Snails and crabs may crawl about the bottom, stay put or even float, but fish can do all these things, and also enjoy the freedom of the open waters. They have a well-developed sense of sight, some even with colour vision, and they have a keen sense of smell, facilities put to good use in finding food and evading enemies. In addition to these they have a lateral line of sensory cells – easily seen as a coloured line on many of the fish found on the fishmonger's slab. These cells help the fish to detect movements and vibrations in the water.

Fish which live on or near the sea-bed are known as *demersal*, while those inhabiting the open waters are of the sea-going *pelagic* species. In science, fish are divided into three classes; the primitive hagfish and lampreys; the cartilaginous sharks, skates and rays; and the 20,000 species of bony fishes.

The mackerel with its beautifully streamlined shape, is a typical example of a pelagic bony fish. Its bluntly rounded shape at the head end tapers towards the tail, providing the least resistance to the water and reducing turbulence. This reduced friction is necessary if the fish is to achieve a fair speed through the dense medium of water. Every feature of the fish is designed to produce a surface which offers no irregularities or pro-truberances to create turbulence. Its mouth closes tight, its eyes and gill covers fit flush, and the body fins operate from slight depressions into which they may fold almost flat when the fish is operating at maximum speed. The body scales are small and smooth, and the whole surface is covered with a mucus slime which helps to grease its passage through the water. The resultant speed allows it not only to chase and capture prey efficiently, but also to escape from trouble.

The fish's fins serve important and distinctive purposes. The dorsal and anal fins are concerned with stabilising the body and countering any tendency to yaw. The paired fins behind and below the head are surfaces controlling pitch and elevation, and of course the tail fin is the propulsion unit, the fishy version of a boat's screw. In order to maintain position at a given depth, many bony fish have trim tanks – controllable buoyancy chambers known as air bladders, or sometimes swim bladders.

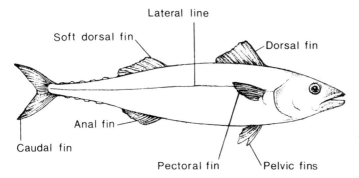

Mackerel hunt in open water, but a lot of bony fish live on the bottom in shallow water. These demersal fish, of which the plaice is a good example, have evolved a flat shape which is more suited to their life-style. In order to blend inconspicuously with their background, they lie on their sides. This would render one eye inoperative, but in the course of time the fish's head – eyes and all – has altered its position in such a way that both eyes look upwards from the exposed side. While the fish's underside is more or less white, where it will be out of sight

Unsuspecting tube-worm about to be attacked by a hunting plaice.

anyway, the upper, exposed surface is camouflaged with colours, spots and blotches to suit the sandy or muddy background. In order to swim, the fish undulates in a wave-form, skimming and gliding close to the bottom. Since its prey is usually worms, crustaceans and molluscs, it has no requirement for speed in hunting, and to evade its own enemies it relies on camouflaged stillness. It has also perfected the trick of wiggling its marginal fins at the last moment before it settles, throwing up a flurry of sand which then drops to provide extra cover on its exposed side.

Yet another life-style is demonstrated by the gurnards, fish which rely on neither speed nor camouflage to thwart their attackers, but protect themselves with bony plates and fearsome spines. These are remarkable fishes which 'walk' over the sea bed in search of food. Two or three of the rays of their pectoral fins are extra long, forming free-ranging feelers which probe and explore amongst the weed and stones, a process which may be seen in action in any aquarium.

The most remarkable of all feeding techniques must surely be that of the cunning angler fish. This, too, has a precociously developed ray, one only, the first ray of the dorsal fin, which has migrated to the front of the fish's head and is canted forward in such a way that it projects ahead of the mouth. Attached to the end of this 'rod' there is a little rag of tissue which acts as bait – so the fish is fully equipped with a fishing rod and a lure as well.

Lying on the bottom, well camouflaged against the gravel, the angler flicks the lure about to simulate the jerking movement of a small sea creature. When a suitable prey fish comes to investigate, the lure is flicked downwards, towards the angler's mouth. The prey moves in to take the lure, which is then withdrawn to safety as the truly enormous gape of the angler fish opens wide to allow an inrush of water, complete with the unfortunate prey. The angler may grow to a metre in length, and while it may not appear to us the most beautiful fish in the sea, it nevertheless serves us well under a false name. Many anglers are caught in trawl nets, and the dense white flesh of the tail end is cut into small pieces to arrive on the restaurant table in the guise of 'scampi'.

Like most bony fish, the angler reproduces by spawning, when the female produces a mass of eggs, gathered together in a mucus raft, and fertilised externally by the male's sperm, or milt. The extraordinary number of eggs produced by fishes, often many million from a single female, helps to swell the seasonal ranks of the plankton animals, and, as is the case with all animals which produce large numbers, most of the young are destined for an early death as food for other, larger, fishes.

This reproductive generosity is not at all characteristic of the other great class of fishes, the Selachians, which includes sharks, dogfish, skates and rays. The female's eggs are fertilised internally by the male in an act of sexual union, and the resulting little fish lives for some time on a diet of yolk in the egg-sac before venturing into the open sea. Another major difference between these fish and the bony fishes is that they have no air bladder. They maintain a slightly negative buoyancy which can be overcome with ease when the powerful tail thrusts the fish forward.

Above Rays spend most of their time on the sea bed, but are able to 'fly' through the water using their enlarged pectoral fins as wings. *Below left* The male shark's 'claspers', grooved appendages of the pelvic fins which, when inserted into the female's cloaca, provide a route for the seminal fluid.

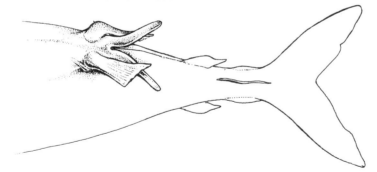

The rays, skates and dogfish spend most of their time on the sea-bed, hunting crustaceans, molluscs and other fish. The skates and rays are specially flattened for bottom living, with greatly enlarged pectoral fins which serve to flap the fish through the water in a manner which is closer to flying than swimming. They seem sluggish, but are perfectly able to move quickly when they are after prey, which they smother with their bodies, feeding at leisure by way of a mouth slit placed well back under the head.

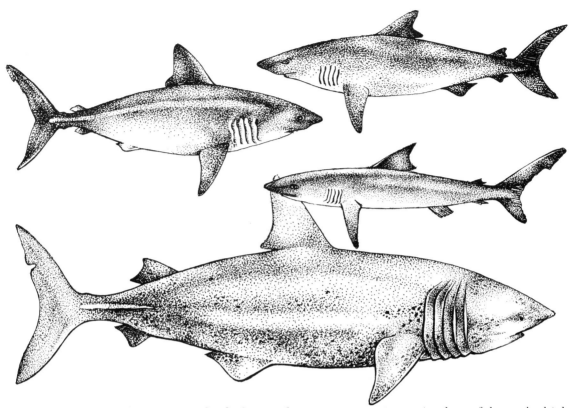

Common British sharks.
Top to bottom Blue, porbeagle, mako and basking.

Sharks have a fearsome reputation as 'wolves of the sea' which is hardly deserved. But some of them, for instance the blue shark, which is found commonly off the coasts of the south-west, are certainly voracious predators. Built for speed, they have a powerful tail fin, and their streamlining is carried to the extent that the mouth is tucked away underneath so that the blunt snout can present a smooth hydrodynamic entry to the water. The mouth is full of sharp teeth, which are modified versions, enlarged and erect, of the scales which cover the whole body. In effect the shark's outer skin is tucked back to form a mouth, and in the tucked-in area, the scales present themselves as teeth. The teeth project back slightly into the mouth to make it even more difficult for the prey to get out.

However, for all its reputation, you are unlikely to have your leg chopped off at one stroke by a blue shark, and the self-satisfaction of the shark-anglers at having conquered this terror of the sea is somewhat exaggerated. You are even less likely to lose a leg to the magnificent basking shark, because it feeds entirely on plankton. It cruises at the surface, its open

Cruising at the surface with open mouth, the giant basking shark sieves plankton from great quantities of sea water.

mouth sampling thousands of tons of seawater every hour, sieving the plankton out with the fine-tooth comb of its gill rakers. A placid and inoffensive creature (so long as you are not a member of the plankton community) it is a common sight off western coasts in the summer. Feeding typically close inshore, the tip of its snout and those two lazy fins, dorsal and tail, showing just above the surface, this shark is guaranteed to clear a beach of bathers in no time. Yet skin-divers can swim close to the great fish which may be as much as twelve metres long, without difficulty, if they behave with caution. The only time when a basker may become dangerous is when it 'sounds' in a panic, when its sheer bulk and lashing tail may capsize the small boat which may have surprised it. Like the other selachians, this fish has no swim bladder but it maintains its surface station by manipulating the buoyancy of its massive, oily liver.

Often you will see a party of herring gulls on the water where a basking shark is performing its lazy circles. Presumably they derive some benefit from this activity, though they never seem to be actively feeding at the time. On other occasions, when for example a mackerel shoal is chasing hordes of tiny fish at the surface, the gulls will join in the hunt. Gulls are opportunist feeders, having a go at anything, and they are the common companions of any trip round the bay. In summer there may be terns fishing the surface waters, too. Common and arctic terns, with their swallow-tails, or sandwich terns, with

their heavier bodies and yellow-tipped bills, all patrol the inshore waters, ready to pounce on a surface titbit.

The most spectacular 'pouncer' is the gannet, which plunge-dives on its prey, a mackerel perhaps, from a great height. First marking its chosen prey from the air, it closes its wings to accelerate headlong. Specially adapted for this activity, with forward vision, slit nostrils and protective air-sacs forming a double breast, gannets strike the surface with great force, sending up a tremendous splash and continuing the dive in an underwater chase using feet and wings. The catch may be swallowed underwater or it may be brought to the surface. Usually the dive is brief and the bird rises, takes off, then circles to dive again. Though you may see them close inshore, especially in stormy weather, gannets usually hunt far out to sea. Whiter-than-white, their long wings tipped with black, they are as big as a turkey and easily recognised.

Sea ducks enjoy the feeding in sheltered coastal waters outside the breeding season, and they are common enough. Shy birds, seldom ashore, they group together on the water in rafts which may consist of hundreds of birds. They are divers, swimming to the sea-bed for molluscs and crustaceans in dives which usually last about half a minute. Common scoters are likely sightings. The drakes have a striking glossy black plumage, with a prominent yellow patch on a black bill, but you will be lucky to see that; usually they take off and fly away in a party long before you get close to them. On the water they have a buoyant posture, but when alarmed they are able to sink down and make themselves inconspicuous.

Other diving birds, like shags and cormorants, tend to maintain this sunken posture, swimming with what any sailorman would regard as a dangerously low freeboard – not much ship above the surface! But there is a real advantage here for the birds. As divers, they are more efficient when they carry less surface air down with them, so they have plumage which is intentionally less waterproof than that of most birds. Whereas ducks, for instance, retain a layer of warmed air between their skin and their plumage, shags and cormorants use the wet-suit principle employed by human divers. The disadvantage is that they do get wet, and therefore need to dry their plumage after diving, in order to regain full flight capability and to restore the thermal qualities of their feathers.

In spring, both shags and cormorants are common coastal breeding species, though their requirements differ significantly.

Shags swim low in the water and dive in jack-knife fashion to chase fish, propelled by webbed feet.

The cormorants choose to nest sociably in colonies on rocky slopes, whereas the shags nest in solitary isolation in some dark crevice or cranny. Both feed on the plentiful shoal-water fish like pollack and wrasse, but outside the breeding season cormorants tend to forsake the coast for the more sheltered waters of the estuaries.

Seals are predators on fish, too. They tend to find themselves a convenient resting place, a sand-bank in the case of common seals or a smooth and easily reached rocky ledge in the case of the grey seals, and go fishing when the rising tide forces them out of bed. We once watched a cow grey seal surface in shallow water, with a large flatfish gripped in her teeth. Lying comfortably in an upright position in the water, she proceeded to eat it at leisure, holding the carcass between her two mobile front flippers just as if she were sitting at table.

As divers, seals are well adapted. They can stay under water for several minutes of active chasing, using the full power of their hind flippers, but if they simply choose to sleep on the sea bed they have the facility of reducing their heart rate – and therefore their rate of oxygen use – in order to rest undisturbed for twenty minutes or so. When the level of oxygen in the blood drops too low, they rise gently to the surface to flush out the system and take in a fresh charge of air. Then they sink slowly to the bottom again – all this without waking up! As a warm-blooded mammal, the seal's provision for heat insulation includes a thick pelt of fur outside and a solid layer of blubber inside the skin.

No one is likely to mistake a seal for a fish, yet whales of all sorts are frequently misidentified in this way. Unlike the seals, which spend a great deal of time ashore (and indeed must come ashore to drop their pups) the whales are mammals which spend their whole life immersed in the sea. They have forsaken any kind of fur coat (which has the disadvantage that it eventually becomes waterlogged) because they would have no way of regularly drying it as the seal does. Instead they rely on the insulating properties of blubber to maintain their body temperature. In shape they are very fish-like, for the excellent reason that the fish shape is the most efficient form for travelling in water. Like fish and seals, they drive themselves by means of tail fins, but in the case of the whales these are attached horizontally, so that the forward motion through the water is achieved by an up and down stroke instead of the fish-like side to side movement.

Top In courtship plumage, the cormorant has white throat and thigh patches, while the shag sports a crest. *Bottom* The cormorant (right) is larger and heavier-necked, the shag having a more elegant snake-like neck. If in doubt, count the tail feathers. Cormorants have fourteen, shags twelve.

Whales of British waters.
Top to bottom Killer, pilot, dolphin and porpoise.

Whales (known in biological parlance as Cetaceans) come in two kinds, those which have teeth and are active predators on fish, birds, seals and other whales; and whalebone whales which trawl the sea with open mouths, sieving shrimps from enormous quantities of water. Off the coast of Britain we are most likely to see the smaller whales, the dolphins and porpoises, although killer whales and pilot whales are not infrequent visitors. Fishermen in west Cornwall like to tell of the days on which a killer whale, longer than the six-metre crabber the men are working in, comes alongside and raises a beady eye to see what is going on. Though the danger from killers is much exaggerated, it is only prudent to give them a wide berth.

Whales have small eyes, since their principal fish-catching sense is not vision but a form of echo-location, in which they listen for the returning echo of sound signals which they themselves originate. If you ever find yourself diving in the midst of a school of cetaceans, as one of us has done, you will hear a continuous rain of high-frequency whistles and clicks, increasing in intensity as they approach through the murky water – an unnerving experience when the sound is made by a carnivorous mammal larger than yourself.

Echo-location, using a visual display, is one of the prime techniques used nowadays by another fish-hunting mammal, Man. Ever since the year dot, man has been a keen fisherman, and has played a full part in harvesting the bounty of the sea. Harvesting is, perhaps, a wrong word to use, since sea fishing is more a matter of hunting, there being no question of sowing that we may reap. We have come a long way since the days when Mesolithic man fashioned harpoons and bone hooks and hammered shellfish off rocks with stones. But, apart from certain shellfish, notably the oyster, we have not yet cracked the problem of farming the fertile acres of the sea commercially. Though the fishing industry today is highly sophisticated, it is still based on the crudest principles of scoop, scrape, entangle and snare. The vessels used for the job have changed little, though their propulsion units and gear have changed a lot. The most significant change came at the turn of the century, when steam tugs were first used to tow a fleet of sailing trawlers to the fishing grounds (thus increasing their working time) and then to bring them home again to market. By the end of World War I most large fishing boats operated under steam of their own, while the inshore day boats were still dependent on sail. Nowadays, when diesel engines reign supreme, the only sails to be seen are the occasional steadying mizzen, apart from delightful anachronisms like the Helford River oyster fleet, which must, by law, fish under sail alone, thus providing us with a taste of bygone beauty.

Fishing boats come in all shapes and sizes, tested in severe conditions and adapted to their different jobs in much the same way as their prey have evolved for their way of life. Open boats, up to about thirteen metres in length, crabbers and long-liners, often working from open beaches or natural harbours, operate close inshore on a daily basis for shellfish, or for ling and conger, ray and turbot. Much larger, and vastly more expensive, purse-seiners work away for days at a time, surrounding whole shoals with their nets, then storing the catch in chilled seawater tanks. However, the most developed of the fishing vessels is the trawler. In biological terms, it is a voracious predator – highly seaworthy, very powerful and with a high load capacity. A typical Newlyn vessel, the *Rose of Sharon*, is built for dual purpose working, side or stern trawling. Twenty metres in overall length, she works the Western Approaches from Start

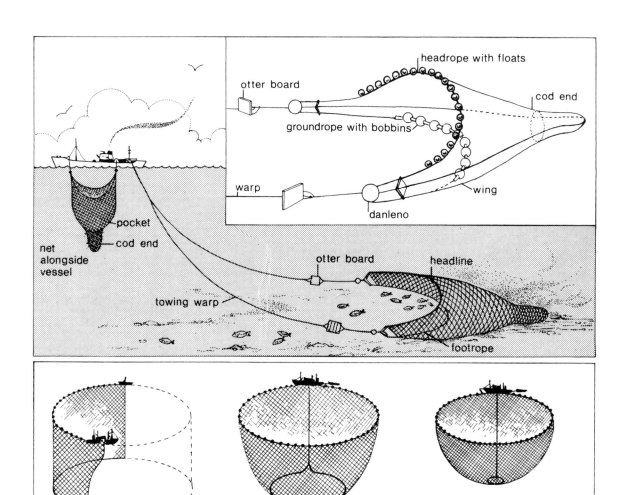

otter board

headrope with floats

cod end

groundrope with bobbins

warp

wing

danleno

pocket

cod end

net
alongside
vessel

towing warp

otter board

headline

footrope

Top Trawlers tow an open-mouthed net along the sea-bed to disturb and engulf demersal fish.
Middle Purse-seiners 'bag' a sample of surface water for pelagic fish.
Right Long-liners catch bottom fish like ling with baited hook and line.
Page 25 In repose, the spotted, upper surface of the plaice provides it with good camouflage.

buoy

snood with
baited hook

anchor

Above The surface waters of the sea provide a home for a great community of microscopic life – the passively drifting plankton plants and animals.

Right Minute plants like the dinoflagellate *Ceratium* carry whip-like processes which counteract sinking and help maintain the organism near the surface.

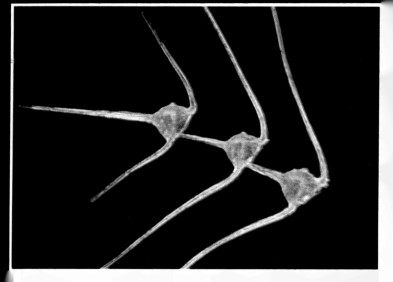

Two of the many bird species which make a living from the sea. Gannets are plunge-divers, hunting surface fish such as mackerel and using high-power binocular vision. Common scoters are sea-ducks, diving in shallow inshore waters for shellfish.

Point to Scilly, fishing mackerel in winter and 'flats' in the summer. Just forward of her wheelhouse is a powerful winch with a thirteen-ton pull, the sort of power needed to deal with heavy trawl warps towing a net that may be as big as a rugby pitch along the sea bed for three or four hours at a time. The mouth of the trawl is kept open by a row of floats along its top edge and by the otter boards, whose movement through the water splays the net out sideways. At the base of the net, a heavy foot chain stirs up the sea bed, disturbing demersal fish which fall into the mouth of the net and are swept down to the cod end. The trawl net is towed by heavy lines – warps – which are led from the winch by way of heavy metal supports – gallows – at the side or the stern of the vessel (hence 'side' or 'stern' trawlers).

When the trawling period is over, the vessel heaves to and the big winch turns, hauling in the warps. When the otter boards surface they are secured to the gallows, then the mouth end of the net is piled on the deck. When the cod end breaks the surface, bloated with an assortment of fish, kittiwakes and fulmars swarm in to enjoy their share of the catch. Large quantities of undersized fish and unwanted species are destined to be swept overboard when the catch is sorted. For the naturalist, the major interest of a trip with a trawling crew is the excitement of sorting through this 'trash'.

If the trawling has been close inshore there will be oarweed fronds, swarming with life, worms, molluscs and seamats, and there will be sea urchins and starfish and brittlestars a-plenty. The deeper you go, the more surprises there are in the catch – enough to keep you occupied for hours. Never pass up the chance to join a trawlerman for a day, for there is almost nothing to beat the excitement of the random collection of sea life pouring over the ship's deck when the crewman releases the cod-end knot!

Beam trawlers tow by way of massive outboard booms which are stayed to the mainmast and pull two trawls, one each side. They may work for demersal fish or, more likely, for scallops, in which case they use a trawl made of steel mesh, with the foot chain replaced by a fixed metal bar with teeth, which digs up the top layer of sand, scallops and all.

In terms of efficiency, trawlers work best when they act as a fleet, locating and maintaining contact with the fish shoals, so that while the day-boat men may still work from coves and harbours, sometimes little more than natural shelters, the

Page 28 Horse-mackerel, typical plankton-hunting surface fish. *Below* Crewman releases the cod-end for a cascade of fish to land on the trawler's deck.

Unloading fish boxes from the hold, Ullapool Quay, Scotland. A modern stern trawler registered in Lowestoft. Fulmars waiting for rich pickings when the trawl is hauled in.

heavier end of the industry has concentrated on the relatively few places which have developed the necessary specialised facilities to serve large fleets. A man-made breakwater and long quays complete with ice factory, fish market and rail terminal, are the order of the day. Most capital investment is concentrated on the 'distant water' ports like Hull and Grimsby. At Hull, where until recently half the fish caught by British trawlers was landed, there is a quay a mile in length, yet in the past it has been not an inch too long. But fortunes in the fishing industry, like the fish stocks themselves, are liable to violent change, and because of overfishing in the arctic, there are big trawlers lying idle in many east coast ports.

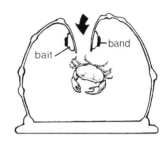

The pattern of fishing varies greatly with the coastal geography. In the north-east, the fish market demonstrates endless rows of cod and haddock. At Lowestoft, the fish boxes are filled with plaice. By contrast, at Brixham or Plymouth or Newlyn in the south-west, the landings on a single day may encompass an astonishing variety of species. On a successful July day in Newlyn the auctioneers may sell over thirty species including, as a random sample, ling, bass, conger, spurdog, dogfish, tope, pouting, cuckoo and thornback ray, turbot, brill, angler fish, pollack, bream, red and tub gurnard, angel fish, saithe, cod, plaice, lemon and dover sole, megrim, hake, haddock, John Dory, porbeagle and blue shark, also molluscs like squid and octopus. And not to mention the crabs, crawfish, lobsters and scallops that are landed in the same port but marketed elsewhere. Of some 160 sea fishes regarded by the Ministry of Agriculture and Fisheries as common in British waters, only thirty-four are listed as commercially edible, while many others remain to have their day when prejudices can be overcome. Overcome they will be, as in the past, when dogfish, previously regarded as a pest, found itself on the slab as 'flake' and the tabby-striped catfish (regarded as so ugly that it was skinned at the dockside, before sale) was presented as 'rock-salmon', 'rock turbot' or 'woof'.

Above Traditional 'inkwell' crab pot. (The bait is usually skewered inside the neck of the pot.) The crab smells its way in.
Below Size comparison between the scampi prawn *Nephrops* (left) and the common shrimp (right).

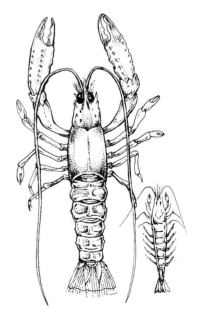

The fish trade, not unreasonably, classifies all fish as either 'round' or 'flat', but it is one of the pleasures of a visit to the fish market to try and unravel the wild intricacies of fish-slab nomenclature. Several species, including catfish and spurdogs, may reach your table as 'rock salmon', and several species lend their flesh to the simulation of 'scampi', a name which belongs by rights to the Norway prawn, *Nephrops*. The lesser spotted dogfish *Scyliorhinus caniculus* may also commonly be known as nursehound, but in Newlyn it is firmly called a mergie, while the Fisheries officers stick out for huss. A saithe is a coalfish is a coley. The textbook angel fish is the fishmonger's monk fish unless you are in Newlyn where it is a fiddler fish. And others say a monk fish is an angler fish anyway. It is a delightful maze!

As rock salmon, the spurdog *Squalus acanthias* is in great demand by the fish and chip trade, now that the traditional round fish species are no longer so plentiful. Grimsby, the centre of the UK dogfish trade, landed 1719 tonnes in 1975, but unfortunately the increased fishing is having a bad effect on stocks, with increased numbers of small fish being taken. Inevitably this heavy fishing of immature stock will accelerate the decline which has been evident since records were begun in 1960. Overfishing has already seen the decline of the herring, whose spawning stock is at a low ebb. And while the sprat has to a certain extent filled the gap, at least in the north-east, one wonders how long sprat stocks can withstand the onslaught.

In the south-west the mackerel is now under siege, and indeed with the herring it is a good example of the fluctuating fortunes of the fishing industry. In the early fifties herrings accounted for 87% of the total pelagic catch. By 1975, in a total catch which remained constant, only 11% were herrings, while sprats, with mackerel coming up close behind, shared 86%. By 1976 herrings were down to 9% of the total, while mackerel at 44% had overtaken the 41% of sprats. Mackerel were heading for a boom or bust, along with the freezer-trawlers which, denied the Icelandic waters, converged on the fish-rich south-west. Well over 95% of the English mackerel catch is taken in the coastal waters of Cornwall and south Devon, mostly in the period October to March. In 1975, for instance, the total West Country catch by both British and foreign vessels was 492 000 tonnes. Whether the stocks can withstand increased fishing remains to be seen, but there has been a dramatic increase in the catch since that time, with a continuing influx of pelagic trawlers from ports outside Devon and Cornwall. Certainly the success of the inshore handline fishermen has been over-shadowed by what must seem a tidal wave of competition.

Fisheries scientists work hard to learn something of the economy of the sea, with a view to knowing how best we may harvest the potentially inexhaustible supplies of protein. But all too often their efforts are hampered by the greed of Man the fisherman, whose concern is often to take everything he can get, without thought of the future.

Footprints in the sand

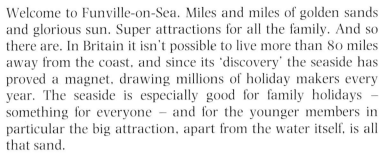

Turnstones are beach birds, living up to their name by turning stones and seaweed in search of edible debris and small animals such as the sandhopper *Talitrus* shown below, much enlarged.

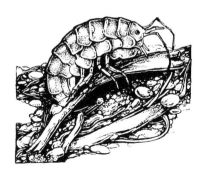

Welcome to Funville-on-Sea. Miles and miles of golden sands and glorious sun. Super attractions for all the family. And so there are. In Britain it isn't possible to live more than 80 miles away from the coast, and since its 'discovery' the seaside has proved a magnet, drawing millions of holiday makers every year. The seaside is especially good for family holidays – something for everyone – and for the younger members in particular the big attraction, apart from the water itself, is all that sand.

Sand is fun. Children enjoy it so much that a sandpit in the garden is a real winner, and every playschool has one. Great stuff for castles, when it's damp; for running through your fingers when it's fine and dry; for digging holes and burying your toes. Sand is fun wherever it is, but the big difference between the stuff in the sandpit and the sand on the beach is that the seaside version is also somebody's home.

On a busy August bank holiday it may seem that people are the only animals on the beach, apart from a handful of raucous dogs and importunate gulls. But the sand is a jungle of wild creatures, if you know where to look. At high-water mark, for instance, there may be a ribbon development of dead plants, freshly thrown up by the receding tide, and this will support a thriving population of sand-hoppers. *Talitrus saltator* is the one most likely to be spotted, but there are over a thousand different species at large. During the day these 'beach fleas' live underground in the dry upper areas of the shore, but at night they come out, to leap about and hunt over the tide-line debris and the lower shore, to see what kind of decaying plant and animal material the tide has brought in.

A surprising number of birds will visit the shore to hunt these sand fleas, and to search among the tide-line debris for flies and molluscs. Turnstones are the most at home here, but pied wagtails and crows come in a close second, while many of the birds more commonly regarded as woodland and garden species will come to try their luck. Robins, blackbirds, starlings and sparrows may all make successful visits to the shore.

On the earth nothing is new. Basic materials are used over and over again, re-appearing in different guises. Sand grains on the beach start life as part of a solid rock. That rock might be solid granite or gleaming chalk; or the wheel may turn full circle when sandstone, a rock made from compacted sand grains, is again broken down to its component parts. The sea, of course, is the giant which crushes rock into sand, but in the case of sandstone, or other soft substrates like shale, slate or chalk, the process of breakdown may be aided by molluscs which are, literally, boring. Several species do it – the common piddock is a good example.

In the larval stage of its life the piddock free-floats in the plankton but, settling on a suitably soft rock, it sets to work with its specially designed drilling shells. With a see-saw action and rotating the valves through a right-angle, rows of fine teeth bore into the rock. Quite a small hole is made, for the animal itself is small at this stage. But once inside and safe from predators, it grows, and in growing enlarges the chamber, until it may reach back thirty centimetres into the rock. For the rest of its life it inhabits this self-made cave, reaching out to feed on passing titbits when the tide is in. When, in due course, it dies, the sea is able to reach an eroding finger into the little cavern and exploit it further, taking advantage of the weak spot engineered by the piddock.

There's no doubt that the principal demolition agency is the sea, when, in destructive vein, it acts directly on the rock of the land. At the base of cliffs, for example, waves may cut into the rock until an overhang is formed, and eventually rocks fall. This tumble of rocks is then pounded and crushed by the waves, so that boulders become large pebbles, then smaller pebbles, until they become small and light enough for the waves to pick up and carry away. During the journey from cliff to beach resting-place, a lot of wear and tear goes on, so the sand grains which survive to build our beaches need to be made of pretty hard and enduring stuff.

Waves, which are the most important agents in trans-porting sand around the coast are formed far out at sea by the action of the wind. On the beach we see them in many different shapes and sizes; as gentle ripples or crashing breakers as they expend their energy on the shore. But in the open sea, they have a circular form, developed as the wind drives individual particles of water in oscillatory movements. The water particles move round and round, without actually moving forward very much, and the orbits which they perform have several different characteristics which, combined, account for the state of the sea on a particular day. In deep water, the sea bed does not impinge on the circular motions; even the highest waves of a stormy sea leave the deep sea bed undisturbed. But as the swells approach land and the water becomes shallower, the influence of the sea bed becomes felt, so

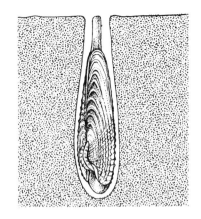

Piddocks bore into soft rock, then enlarge the burrow as they grow. *Below* Sandstone suits them very well, and as time passes the rock is fast eroded by the action of the sea aided by the molluscs.

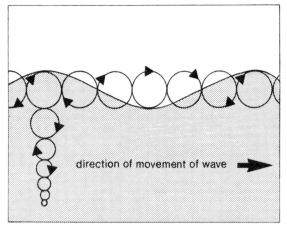

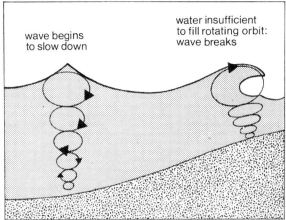

wave begins
to slow down

water insufficient
to fill rotating orbit:
wave breaks

direction of movement of wave ➡

Page 37, top left Heart urchin or sea potato. The tuft of tube feet on the upper surface line the burrow and reach up for food.
Top right Heart urchin burrowing into wet sand.
Bottom Burrowing starfish digging into safety underground.

that the water particles which previously moved in circular fashion take on an elliptical form, gradually flattening towards the bottom, until at the sea bed itself the movement is largely to and fro. This friction between sea bed and the moving water stirs up the sediments lying offshore, and thus the waves pick up their load. Sand which is raised from offshore banks is then carried by the moving waves; and whether it is then deposited to form a sandy beach, or used like a scouring powder by waves determined to erode yet more land, depends largely on the prevailing winds and the configuration of the coast.

On a particular piece of coastline the wind, and therefore the waves, approach most often from a particular direction. In the south of England, for instance, the prevailing winds are south-westerlies. They are responsible for moving beach materials in the general direction of west to east, by the all-important process known as *longshore drift*. Longshore drift operates by virtue of the fact that waves usually approach the shore at an angle. The waves, with their cargo of sand, follow this diagonal line of approach up the beach – the action of

Longshore drift:
A Waves driven obliquely by wind and current against shore.
B Debris swept up beach in a curve.
C Wave subsides, material is dragged back and is thus carried along the coast in a zig-zag path.

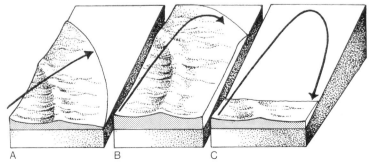

A   B   C

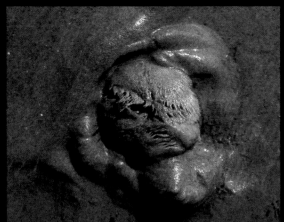

'swash'; but when the water of the 'backwash' returns to the sea, it naturally follows the line of least resistance and runs back at right-angles to the shore – straight down the beach. This kind of action, wave after wave, ensures that any beach material being carried is moved along – zig-zag fashion – in the direction of the prevailing wind and waves.

The balance of power between the swash and the backwash decides whether a beach is being built up or gradually removed. Out at sea, the speed of individual water particles is less than the speed of the wave as a whole, but as the wave is slowed down by contact with the sea bed the orbital velocity catches up until, at the crest, it is the same as the speed of the wave itself. The wave inevitably spills over, or breaks. Waves must break when they reach the shore, and it is the manner of this breaking which determines whether the wave will be 'constructive', with the swash most powerful, or of a 'destructive' nature. In calm conditions and in sheltered places waves spill over gently, pushing sand up the beach, and the energy of the backwash is soon dissipated by percolation through the sand and shingle. These are constructive waves. In storm conditions and on exposed coasts, when strong winds allow steep waves to develop, these reach the shore as plunging breakers which fall almost vertically on to the beach, producing a very strong backwash – the 'undertow' – which can be so dangerous to bathers. These waves are destructive.

Constructive waves are best for bathers, surfers in particular, who ride ashore by manipulating the wave energy for their own purpose. For the animals which live in the region of the beach it is clearly important that constructive waves should bring in sand to build their home environment, and the quality of that sand is also significant. The quality of sand matters most to the inhabitants when the tide is out, because it is then that this unlikely medium must provide shelter, water, oxygen and food for worms and starfish and razorshells and cockles. For the animals, the stuff of which the sand is made – the inorganic rock – does not matter much, but the size of the particles does. Just like the terrestrial soil, the coarser the grains of sand the less they are able to hold water around themselves by capillary action. The swash and backwash of the waves achieves some grading of material on the beach, the larger, heavier particles being carried furthest up the beach while the weaker backwash drags back to the bottom only the finer sands and sediments. It is in these lower regions, where the sand

Page 38, top left Common starfish sizing up a bed of mussels.
Top right Queen scallops escape from attack using jet propulsion when they close their valves violently by muscle action.
Bottom The siphon of the netted dog whelk sniffs out its carrion dinner, in this case a dead shore crab.

Surfers ride ashore on a spilling breaker, using part of the wave's energy for free transport.

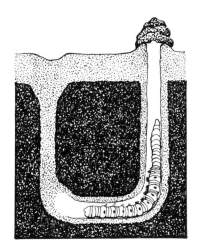

retains most moisture, that the greatest concentrations of animals are found.

The sandy beach is not an easy place in which to live, but there is a twice-daily delivery of fresh food, on each tidal inundation, and where there is an available food source you can depend on the ingenuity of animals to take advantage of it. There are various reasons why the hungry animal should not just sit on the beach and wait for dinner time. The heat of the sun, driving cold rain, the pounding force of the waves, and passing predators are just a few of them. But the effects of sun, wind and waves are only skin deep. If you can dig down just a few inches you are in a relatively stable environment, with more or less constant salinity and temperature. So the most elegant way of avoiding these problems is to burrow under the sand during unfavourable periods, migrating up and down in order to feed or to hide. Burrowing animals have a choice of several ways of feeding. They may reach out and sample the passing plankton; they may scour the surface deposits left by the passage of the tides; they may sieve the goodness out of the sand itself; or they may hunt other burrowers. One way or another, then, the wet sand supports a vast community of worms, crustaceans, molluscs, echinoderms and burrowing fishes, each with its own particular method of feeding.

The lugworm is a good example, swallowing the sand it lives in, sorting and digesting the organic debris, and rejecting the inedible portion. Not surprisingly, it has a lot of material to reject, and this is thrown up on the surface in worm-like sand casts. These characteristic sand piles are easy to find when the tide is out, and are a sure indication that there is a lugworm underneath. They are often black, revealing the presence of a sulphide-rich layer in the sand, where most of the oxygen has been used up by the sand inhabitants. A few inches away from the sand cast there will be a shallow depression in the surface, and this marks the entrance to the worm's U-shaped gallery. When the tide comes in, it imports a fresh supply of sand and food particles which fill the depression, and the worm then gets to work swallowing it. If all goes well, the worm will remain in the same burrow for a long time, although it is an insubstantial construction, the walls stiffened with mucus. The worm itself is fat and juicy, and can be anything up to twenty centimetres long. Fish certainly regard it as a prize, and that is why countless thousands of lugworms are dug up for use as bait by anglers every year.

The other marine worms which are very common on the lower reaches of a sandy beach are the tube worms, which build themselves a home out of the only material available to them, the sand itself. These 'sand masons' secrete a sticky mucus which is the binding material used in constructing a kind of sheath which allows the worm to move up and down in sympathy with the tidal rhythm. Down below, it has a measure of safety from the elements and its predators. Reaching up, when the tide is in, it can extend its tentacles and gills to collect food particles from the immediate area of its front door. When the tide recedes, only the top end of the sandy tube remains visible. Sometimes, after a storm, large numbers of the tubes may be wrenched from the sand and thrown up on the tide line. They are well worth examining closely, revealing the most painstaking efforts of the builder.

Page 40 Lugworm in its burrow, head end depression to the left, tail end casting to the right. The photograph shows the tell-tale signs of a lugworm-infested beach. Food particles are swallowed, along with a lot of sand from the depression and the sand is ejected soon afterwards in the form of a worm-shaped cast.

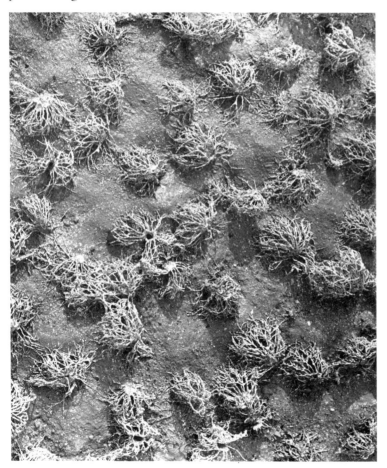

Above The sand mason constructs its protective tube from the only building material available to it – sand. When the tide is in, its tentacles extend to sweep the water for food particles.
Left When the tide recedes, the worm withdraws down to safety, leaving only the frilly top of the tube to mark its home.

The fragile test (skeleton) of the heart urchin. The rows of holes through which the tube feet emerge can be clearly seen.

Another marvel of construction is the fragile 'shell' of the sea potato, or heart urchin *Echinocardium*, which is often found at the tide's edge after its owner has died. A white and rather skull-like capsule, the hollow skeleton (or test) is marked with five rows of holes from which, in life, emerged the hydraulic tube-feet of the animal. These five rays are characteristic of all the sea urchins and the closely related starfish. Hold the empty test up to the sky to see the full beauty of the radiating arms.

While the empty test is superficially similar to that of the edible urchin *Echinus*, whose beautifully coloured globe is so sadly offered for sale by seaside shell shops, the life style of the sea potato is very different. While *Echinus* grazes on rocks and seaweed, *Echinocardium* burrows in sand. To find it you must go to the lower shore at low water. Look in the sort of places where lugworms advertise themselves so clearly, for a star-shaped depression in the sand. Find one with clear, recently formed markings. Dig down gently with your fingers, anything up to twenty centimetres. Unlike the edible sea urchin, its spines are soft, almost furry, so there is no danger of pricking your fingers! But be gentle, it is only too easy to crush the shell.

Once you have the sandy coloured creature in your hands, have a close look at the spines. Some are spade-shaped – specially modified as digging tools. And notice that the spines are 'laid back' against the test, all facing the same way, as a further aid to burrowing. The five-rayed arrangement of holes in the test allows the tube feet to emerge and do their various jobs, helping with respiration, food collection and delivery and disposal of waste. Since the animal lives in its burrow a fair distance from the surface, some of the hydraulic tubes have to reach nearly ten centimetres by way of a chimney to search about for food particles. Put the urchin back into its burrow after you have examined it and cover it carefully with sand. If you simply leave it on the surface in the open air, it cannot burrow fast enough to escape marauding gulls. It takes perhaps fifteen minutes to burrow out of sight.

The burrowing starfish, *Astropecten*, is a close relative of the sea potato, although its starfish shape is superficially very different. But once you remember the five-rayed symmetry which is typical of echinoderms, the relationship becomes more credible. *Astropecten* burrows down just beneath the surface, but maintains a surface presence with the tips of its arms. Instead of feeding on chance particles of food, it is an active predator, seizing small molluscs and swallowing them whole.

Since the bivalve shellfish have to gape open at intervals, even when they are in someone else's stomach, the starfish waits its time, letting its digestive juices do their dirty work when the shell relaxes. In due course the central disc shows itself above the sand and rejects the cleaned-out shells.

A quite different process is used by the more familiar starfish of the rocky shore, *Asterias*, which uses its sucker feet to force open the mollusc shells, then protrudes its stomach into the shell to enjoy the shellfish *in situ*. The burrowing starfish eats its meal in the secrecy of its sandy hideout, but in any case its tube feet are pointed for burrowing, and it would be hard put to clamber about on rocks the way *Asterias* does. *Astropecten* does not need to be covered after you have looked at it. Put it on wet soft sand, at low water. Its finger tips flex and probe. Slowly, it sinks below the surface as you watch, leaving a faintly outlined star in the sand to mark its lair.

The commonest of all shore animals are the molluscs, whose empty shells litter the surface of many beaches. One of the most successful of all animal groups, molluscs crawl, burrow, float and swim both by land and by sea all over the world, but the greatest concentrations of them live in the sand, out of sight, protected by their armour plating. Broadly speaking, the gastropod molluscs – the single-valved snails – live on rocky shores or on the seaweeds, and the under-sand creatures belong to a different class, the Bivalvia. Bivalve molluscs live in sand, wood or rock (like the piddocks) or by mooring themselves to some sympathetic anchorage. Under the surface of a sandy beach they live in uncountable numbers. Indeed, one of the many remarkable features of molluscan life is the variety of methods they use to deal with different habitats, along with the astonishing populations they maintain. It is said that an acre of cockle flats in south Wales supports a million and a half cockles!

Yet molluscs are simple creatures. A bag of guts concentrated in a hump and attached to a muscle system which acts as a foot, the whole protected by a calcareous shell formed from a mantle of tissue. They come in all shapes and sizes, from those which creep behind your garden shed to giant squids, by way of cockles and mussels. Cockles are typical of extensive sand flats. Buried just beneath the surface when the tide comes in, they extend two siphons. Water enters through one, is sieved through the gills for the food particles suspended in it, then ejected through the other. The fat cockle feeds on minute plankton plants and suchlike titbits. It is customary for the

Common cockle in typical posture, half-buried in sandy gravel, siphons extended. Drawing water through one, the animal sieves it for food particles, then ejects the waste through the other.

Herring gull 'puddling' for cockles.

gourmet cockle-eater to be told to keep the animal in salt water for a few hours while it rejects any grit or shell particles going through its system, but all the longshore cocklers we've met scorn such niceties. There's nothing quite so delicious as a meaty cockle picked straight from its bed and eaten raw.

Cockles are harvested in enormous numbers, both by people and other animals. When the tide is in they are hunted by starfish and flatfish. When the tide is out the cockle-gatherers rake, scrape and dig for them, filling sacks which may still be carried home on donkey back. In the Isles of Scilly we knew a farmer who took his horse and harrowed the low-tide sand flats for cockles on occasion. In Morecambe Bay, apart from more conventional methods, cocklers are said to tread the sand with their bare feet, to persuade the cockles to come to the surface. This is a technique also used by herring gulls. You often see them standing thoughtfully near the water's edge, then they deliberately stamp their feet, compacting the sand and forcing an uncomfortable worm or cockle to come up for air. But catching the cockle is only half the problem. The shell is thick and strong; the meat is armour-plated for protection. The gull has a simple, if crude, solution. He carries the cockle in his beak to the nearest road or promenade, drops it from a height, then lands to claim the shattered prize.

The bird with the most advanced method for harvesting sea-shells is the oystercatcher. In spite of its name, it mostly hunts cockles and mussels. One of the common shore and lower estuary waders, the black and white 'sea pie' is a familiar sight. And a familiar sound, too, for that matter, with its almost continuous piping and calling. But apart from the striking pied plumage, it has a powerful weapon in its long red beak. Most waders have delicate probing bills, but the oystercatcher is an exception. Its beak is the next best thing to a burglar's jemmy. Patrolling the sand flats in an inch or two of water, he carries his head on one side, looking for the tell-tale open gape of a feeding cockle. If all goes well he can spear it before it senses danger and closes up. Then, most likely he will have severed the adductor muscle and the meat is laid out ready for eating. But even if the bivalve closes on the bird's beak, the oystercatcher is strong enough to force the two halves of the shell apart. If all else fails he has the capacity to penetrate the shell by brute force, with the chisel end of his beak. In the case of mussels, his other favourite dish, he uses somewhat similar methods, stalking the prey in the hope of catching it relaxed and unawares. But faced with a firmly closed shell, the bird turns the mussel over to reveal the flat ventral surface where the shell is weakest, then chisels and scissors to get at the meat.

At least mussels are easy enough to see if they are about, unlike most of the bivalves, which hide themselves under the sand. And while the others do have a certain freedom of movement – they can reach out to the full extent of their feet and then, contracting the muscle violently, roll themselves over the ground – the mussel is anchored securely to the sandy gravel. The mussel's anchor warp – the byssus thread – is made of a sticky substance secreted by a gland in the foot. When you consider that it has to do its job in a variety of temperatures and with alternate wettings and dryings involving both salt and fresh water, the byssus thread is a remarkable substance. The mussel is attached by a cat's cradle of these threads, and as the tidal currents ebb and flow, the shell is free to turn and present the least resistance to the moving sea, but if by a quirk of the weather it becomes inundated with fresh coverings of gravel, it has the facility of up-anchoring and throwing out new lines.

One way and another, the bivalves which make their home in this unlikely sandy environment manage to move as much as they need to. None of them are exactly fast movers, although scallops, for instance, can leap about in the water by closing their valves together so fast that they are jet-propelled for an appreciable distance; far enough to get away from a hungry starfish. The most spectacular disappearing trick, however, is the one performed by the razorshell. The straight smooth shell, often seen lying about on the beach, is beautifully designed to offer least resistance to the sand when the living animal inside decides to pull itself deeper. In the ordinary way, apart from the odd occasion when a storm may uncover it, it will remain out of sight, only a shallow depression at the surface giving a clue to its whereabouts. These depressions are not easy to find, and the best way of discovering the animal is to walk slowly backwards along the wet sand of the lower shore at spring tides. If you do the job properly, then you are rewarded with a sudden squirt of water as you tread near the shell. Dig quickly, and grasp the fast-disappearing shell with the finger and thumb of one hand while you continue revealing it with the other. Like the cockle, it is a suspension feeder, offering short siphons to sample the passing sea-water while the tide is in. Its enormous foot, filling about half the shell, is its insurance against predators. Under attack, it heaves itself vertically downwards, very fast indeed.

Byssus threads anchor the mussel to a pebble, enabling the mollusc to turn into the current in the direction offering least resistance.

A razorshell extends its powerful foot. In a few seconds it will dig in, jerk the shell upright and swiftly burrow down to safety.

Many other shells make a good living in the sand, but all of them depend on having learnt a way of digging into it. Without that facility they would be eaten, either by the fish when the tide was in, or by the birds when the tide was out. The regular incursions of tidal water are vital to the well-being of molluscs. Apart from the charge of nutrients and oxygen brought in with every flooding tide, the water content of the sand is important to the animals because it can affect their ease of burrowing. As a lugworm or a cockle forces its way through the sand, it exerts a pressure on the particles which, if there is not much water present, makes the sand harder and more difficult to penetrate. Sands which contain a lot of water react in the opposite way – they become softer and easier to penetrate. These 'thixotropic' sands, of which quicksands are a most unpopular example, are the most attractive to the sand burrowing animals, and as the tide rises, bringing in more and more water, conditions in the wet sand gradually become more favourable.

Groynes reduce the rate of longshore drift and maintain a resort's most treasured possession – its beach.

No town council is likely to advertise the desirable qualities of quicksands. They are trying to attract people, not lugworms! Firm sand is all-important to places like Bournemouth, Blackpool, Torquay and Teignmouth. Many of the places which boast fine sands occupy bays, because it is in such sheltered situations that the longshore drift, constantly moving sand along the coast, is slowed down or stopped by any obstacle, like a headland. Sand is such a desirable commodity that sometimes Man will erect artificial barriers, called groynes, to curb the natural drifting of sand. These groynes are vital to resorts which would otherwise have their sand moved on. Their effectiveness can be seen by examining the difference in level between sand on the up- and down-drift side of the groyne.

The part of a groyne which is above the level of the high tides makes a useful lee for sunbathers on a windy day, and a good place for jumping-off games, but the portion which extends down into the water also has value for animals and plants. Seaweeds may establish themselves by holding fast to this rare fixed point in an ocean of, to them, uninhabitable sand, and around the seaweeds a whole community of animals may find a living, as we shall see when we look at rocky shores. Acorn barnacles and mussels may attach themselves to the wooden surface of a groyne, and chitons may roam about scavenging. Over a long period of time the voracious gribble may eat the timber away. During the course of its useful life, a groyne will accumulate sand, building it higher and higher until the groyne itself is completely buried and the top sand is always above the reach of the sea. The weeds and mussels which made their home on the artificial reef must then look elsewhere for security.

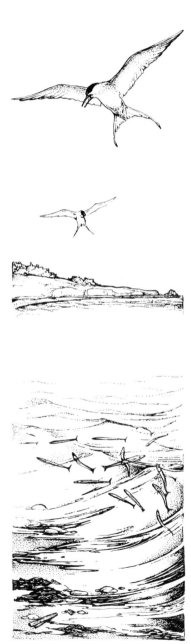

The value placed on sand can be illustrated by the great cost of groyne building. The latest sand traps at Teignmouth, for example, constructed from solid greenheart timber and sunk into the bedrock, cost £1500 each. The extra sand is ideal for Teignmouth, but this process is of course simply a matter of robbing Peter to pay Paul. The sand which is retained by those baulks of timber will not reach the next sandy beach up the coast. Demand for sand exceeds supply, and the supply is diminishing as more and more coastline is protected by sea walls, promenades, and the sandy beaches themselves. If the sea cannot reach the raw coast to batter and gnaw at the rocks new grains of sand cannot begin their life.

In the face of such diminishing supply some authorities, like Bournemouth, have experimented with artificial seaweed – a series of synthetic fronds anchored offshore in the wave-breaking zone. Unlike groynes, this weapon in the beach-loss armoury is not effective against longshore drift, but instead encourages sandy deposits offshore to move towards the beach.

There is great pleasure in wading through the shallow water at the tide's edge, for on a calm, clear day, you will see a great deal of life there. Small hermit crabs scurry about the sea-bed. Shrimps and small fish dart and chase. In the summer there may be terns chattering and calling as they quarter the inshore waters looking for sand eels, picking them daintily off the very surface of the sea, and only barely getting themselves wet. Sand eels, or lance, live at the lowest tide mark, and during

Top Sanderling hunting small stuff along the tide's edge.
Middle Weever fish, with its poisonous dorsal spines.
Bottom Masked crab, half-burrowed.

the infrequent periods of exposure to the air they lie buried under the sand, using their strong lower jaw as a digging tool. They are much eaten by larger fish, by the terns, and by wading birds like sanderling.

Sanderling are plump little waders with short straight bills. Breeding on the barren arctic tundra, far from the seashore, they visit coastal Europe in the winter, although non-breeding birds may well be seen during the summer. Once seen, they are never forgotten, always seeming to be in a panic, dashing along the water's edge like clockwork toys – hardly having time to stop and eat the sandhoppers and small stuff in the backwash before expertly avoiding the swash.

The only drawback to wading in the low-water sandflats is the possibility of an encounter with a weever. Half-buried under the sand, this little fish has modified dorsal spines which can inject a powerful poison. While this poison may be ideal for immobilising a passing shrimp, it can be a very unpleasant experience for a human foot.

At night, when the beach is deserted and the atmosphere is humid, many creatures emerge to enjoy the safety of the dark. Shore crabs come out for the night shift of scavenging, continuing the work done by gulls during the day. Now is the time to make your way down to the water's edge, especially when there is a particularly low tide. You need a torch, and you need to walk quietly, for the night crawlers and scuttlers are shy. The masked crab spends the day time under the sand, out of the way of predatory fish and gulls. During this time he breathes through a tube formed by long antennae which have a double row of stiff hairs, allowing water to be drawn down to the gill chambers. His hind legs are equipped with long claws which are adept at digging and scooping into sand. At night he emerges to explore the lower shore and shallow water areas. Unlike the more conventional crabs, this species does not scuttle 'crabwise' – sideways – and it has a rather endearing way of sitting up and looking interested in life.

Other scavengers show themselves in your torchlight. If there is a piece of dead fish on the sand, look around and under it for the tell-tale humps covering the netted dogwhelk, an active searcher for carrion. They're small, but when their questing siphons sense a suspicion of food, they move along at a surprising speed, just under the surface. One way and another, those acres of bare sand are host to an astonishing range and number of animals.

Rocky shores

The rocky coasts of Britain appear timeless. Unlike shifting sandbanks, bars, shingle ridges and sand dunes, which may present a new picture on every visit to a favourite beach, the rocky shores seem permanent and unchanging. It is only when you witness a cliff fall, or marvel at the unblemished surface of a slate freshly separated from the parent rock, that you realise that erosion is continually happening. For our rocky shores are the product of erosion.

The surface of our island is under constant attack from the elements, but on the coast this attack is intensified, as battle can rage on the open cliff faces as well. Rain, wind, frost and ice are powerful agents of land-based erosion, causing cliffs to slump and blocks to fall, but on the coast the sea adds its weight to the campaign. The sea also plays an important role as an agent of transport, clearing away the fallen debris and so providing destructive waves with renewed opportunities to act upon a fresh cliff face. The sea has several methods of attack. When, in deep water, waves reach to the base of a cliff, the hydraulic pressures exerted can be enough to split open the rock, especially in a well-jointed structure. Air which is trapped in joints and crevices is compressed by the oncoming wave, and the sudden release of pressure caused by the retreating water acts like an explosion, forcing rock to shatter. Rock fragments prised from the cliff in this way, then join the wave's armoury, to be hurled back powerfully, adding insult to injury.

In the shallow water, where waves roll and scrape the loose material over the solid rock of the foreshore, a relatively level rock bench known as a 'wave-cut platform' is formed. The continuous swash and backwash sculpts and smooths the rocks in a relentless effort to reduce the land to a uniform level. But marine erosion is highly selective. The more varied the rocks, the less regular will be the coastline. On the large scale, resistant formations stand out as headlands or islands, while the more easily eroded material gives way to bays. On the local scale, joints, bedding planes and small variations in geology ensure that some rocky foreshores are almost uniform and smooth, whilst others like the marvellous hexagonal blocks of basalt on the Isle of Staffa, or the castellated granite of Land's End, loudly proclaim their geological origins.

A sandy beach is always enjoyable, whether the tide is in or out, but when the tide goes down on a rocky shore, it leaves a landscape which, at first sight, is not very enticing. Seaweeds render the rocks slippery and difficult to negotiate, barnacles

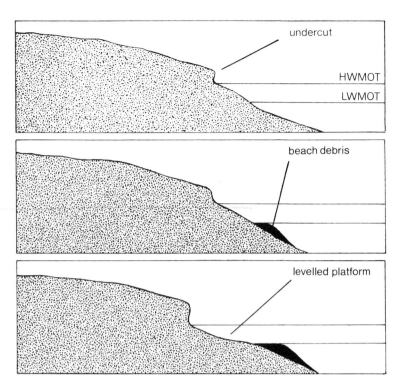

undercut

HWMOT

LWMOT

beach debris

levelled platform

Waves act most powerfully between high and low water mark, in an effort to reduce this area to a level wave-cut platform.

Left Pulpit Rock, Dorset.
Above Fingal's cave, Staffa, where the coast is dominated by the dramatic hexagonal blocks of basalt.

seem to be just waiting to scrape an unwary knee, there are holes to fall into and crevices to trap imprudent feet. Nevertheless for over a century this kind of country has been recognised as a wonderland for wildlife hunters – ranging from the small child seeking crabs for his bucket to the serious seashore naturalist.

During the early nineteenth century, when people were discovering for the first time the joys of running free on the sands and bathing in the health-giving salt water, another kind of joy was being found by people who were caught up in the enthusiasm of a very special naturalist, Philip Henry Gosse. Gosse, born in 1810, grew up with an intense interest in nature. He nurtured this interest during his early career, which took him to America and Canada, first as a clerk then a teacher. His first book, *The Canadian Naturalist*, started him on a lifetime of writing which combined his great talent for descriptive prose with his ability as an artist. His travels abroad were halted by ill-health, and it is fortunate for us that he chose to settle and work in England, in the seaside town of Ilfracombe. His joyous writing opened people's eyes to the wonders of inter-tidal life, and many were able to experience his enthusiasm at first hand as they followed him on conducted tours over the foreshore.

At the head of the procession, like Apollo conducting the Muses, my father strides ahead in an immense wide-awake, loose black coat and trousers, and fisherman's boots, with a collecting-basket in one hand, a staff or prod in the other. Then follow gentlemen of every age . . .
(Edmund Gosse)

Gosse's great achievement was as a populariser, but although he may be the best-known of the Victorian enthusiasts, he was certainly not alone. Mrs. Alfred Gatty, who wrote *British Seaweeds* in 1863, spoke of seaweed collecting as a pursuit

. . . which throws a charm over every sea-place on the coast . . . Only let there be sea, and plenty of low, dark rocks stretching out, peninsular-like, into it, and only let the dinner hour be fixed for high-water time, and the loving disciple asks no more of fate.

In the last quarter of the nineteenth century, interest in the living inhabitants of the rock pools and rugged shores waned in favour of shell collecting and visits to the many shell grottos which sprang up along the coast. Today, happily, more and more people are discovering the pleasure of getting their faces close down to the slippery rocks and shining pools.

Left Text and drawing by Philip Henry Gosse, from *A Year at the Shore*, 1865.

Large prawns swim at freedom through this pool; and a very pleasing sight it is to watch them as they glide gracefully along. The tail-fans are widely dilated, rendering conspicuous the contrasted colours with which they are painted; the jaws are expanded, the feet hanging loosely beneath. Now one rises to the surface almost perpendicularly; then glides down towards the bottom, sweeping up again in a graceful curve. Now he examines the weeds, then shoots under the dark angles of the rock. As he comes up towards me, I stretch out my hand over the water; in an instant he shoots backwards a foot or so; then catching hold of a weed with his feet, and straddling its vertical edge, he remains motionless, gazing up at me with his large prominent eyes, as if in the utmost astonishment.

The range of living things you will find on a rocky shore will be greatly influenced by the amount of shelter available. Clearly a rocky bastion taking the full brunt of the Atlantic attack will have fewer animals and plants to show than the sheltered ledges inside the horns of a great bay. The degree of exposure to sunlight, the salinity, temperature and the effects of man-made pollution will be important factors too, but the most profound influence is that of the tide. Rising and falling twice in a period of just over a day, the tide, with its fortnightly cycle of high-range springs and low-range neaps covers and uncovers the rocks with its periodic gift of nutrient-rich water. At sea, living creatures must solve the problem of visiting or remaining near the surface to enjoy the life-giving properties of sunlight. On the shore, sunlight is always present but plants and animals must suffer the disadvantage that the food-bearing sea is available only on a periodic basis.

Though the inter-tidal area only covers a few metres from top to bottom, it supports a well-defined pattern of plants and animals, ranging from those which exist almost as land animals around the high water mark of spring tides, down to those which only very occasionally show their faces to the open air at the low water mark of the spring tides. Local conditions may vary the limits of this zonation. For instance, on exposed cliffs the effects of waves may send splashes of sea water high up the face to allow some hardy weeds and winkles to survive in what is known as the 'splash zone'. If you examine a sheltered rocky face like, for instance, a man-made embankment along the shore of an estuary, the life-zones are displayed with great

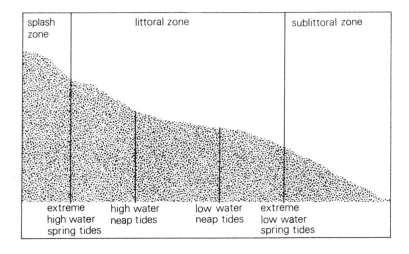

splash zone	littoral zone			sublittoral zone
extreme high water spring tides	high water neap tides	low water neap tides	extreme low water spring tides	

54

ight At low water beadlet
nemones are tightly closed.
Below right When the tide covers
hem, they unfold their tentacles to
rave and attract shrimps and small
sh.

Page 57. top Common sea urchin
Echinus esculentus. Both the spines
nd the hydraulic tube feet are used
n moving over the rock.
Bottom Limpets remain at their
iome base when the tide is out,
inless conditions are very humid.

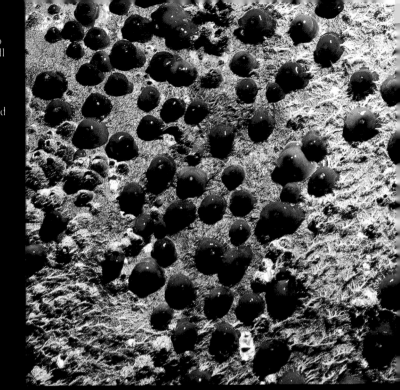

clarity, ranging from the orange lichens which represent the lowest land plants, by way of the rim of black lichen, which looks so uncannily like the effect of oil pollution and is the representative of the uppermost sea plant, down through a whole range of different seaweeds, to the low-water kelps.

The main factor which decides where a species lives is the length of time the rocky shore is exposed to the air. Some seaweeds are adapted to a life lived almost totally in the air, while some can survive only a very occasional period out of the sea. Unlike land plants they have no roots, for the very good reason that there is no soil for them to dig into. Their style is to grip tight to the rocks by means of a 'holdfast', and to derive their nourishment from the surrounding seawater. Like land plants, they contain chlorophyll and are able to form energy-rich sugars by photosynthesis. As *algae*, seaweeds do not flower, but propagate themselves mostly by releasing spores, which free-float in the sea until they form an attachment to some convenient surface. They represent one of the most abundant and under-exploited food sources still left to us on this planet.

Page 58 Hermit crabs take over empty shells, and are often accompanied by sea anemones, a relationship which appears to carry benefits for both creatures (see page 64).

At low water of spring tides, the edge of the kelp forest is exposed.

There are three main groups of seaweeds – green, brown and red. They are found more or less in that order, working down the shore. The seaweeds which dominate the rocky shore are those which derive their brown colour from the pigment *fucoxanthin*. Like most seaweeds, they are best seen on a sheltered shoreline, where they are least bothered by the mechanical effects of wave action. At the top of the shore, around high water mark and as high as the salt spray reaches, is where you will find the dense tufts of channelled wrack. To survive long periods of exposure, its grooved fronds hold moisture while the weed dries and blackens on the surface. Specially adapted to live with only periodic submersion, this plant dies if it is kept underwater experimentally.

The next step down the shore brings you to spiral wrack with its slightly twisted and branched fronds. At the tips of the fronds there may be swollen yellow 'sultanas', the fruiting organs. Then comes bladder wrack, one of the species with great eye-appeal because of its highly poppable air-bladders. These are arranged in pairs, whereas knotted wrack, a weed often found in close company on the middle shore, has somewhat larger bladders which are placed singly. Knotted wrack prefers more sheltered waters, whereas bladder wrack can thrive in the face of a certain amount of wave-thrashing, when the buoyancy of the gas-filled bladders holds the plant up and prevents it from being smashed against the rocks. By floating the weed upwards towards the sun this buoyancy also extends the time available for photosynthesis. Examine the wrack closely and you will often find that some of the 'bladders' are in fact cunningly shaped winkles. Lower down the shore is the home of serrated wrack which has, as its name suggests, toothed margins to the flattened fronds. Look closely at this one and you are very likely, especially if it is a well-established plant, to find the coiled, off-white tubes of *Spirorbis*, one of the bristle worms.

The largest of all the weeds live on the lower shore, the region of the kelps, the *Laminaria* family. Most of the time they are out of sight, underwater, but it is worth going to the shore at an equinox, the time of the lowest spring tides, to enjoy the sight of the edge of the forest of kelps exposed to the air. If the water is clear, allowing sunlight to penetrate and stimulate plant growth, then this weed jungle may stretch away into the submarine distance, perhaps reaching down to fifteen fathoms, the edge of the ocean. The long single fronds of sugary wrack for

Top to bottom Channelled, spiral, bladder and knotted wrack.

example, may form a crumpled ribbon about a metre and a half long. This kelp is the seaweed beloved by amateur weather forecasters as a humidity indicator. As a natural protection against desiccation the plant is slimy and hygroscopic, attracting water, so that if the atmosphere is damp with incipient rain the frond becomes soft and limp. It has the slight disadvantage of a tendency to confirm the weather you have, rather than to forecast the weather that is around the corner! When dry, it reveals a white coating, sweet to taste, as evidence of the presence of a sugar alcohol, mannitol. In fact it has high food value, like many seaweeds, and is still used as horse and pig fodder in places like Iceland and northern France.

Kelps of various shapes crowd the low-water shore, with their leathery straps and stipes, and they represent a potential food source of massive proportions, diminished only by the extreme difficulty of harvesting. Notwithstanding all the problems, these marine weeds have been, and still are, much used in the agricultural and chemical industries. Comparable in food value with meadow hay, weeds such as the tangleweed and the wracks are fed to horses, cattle, sheep and pigs. As fertiliser, great quantities of storm-tossed kelp are spread on coastal fields and gardens. Rich in nitrogen and potassium, kelp is good for potatoes and tomatoes, but its value is restricted by the cost of transport.

As a direct food, seaweed is a staple item of diet in China and Japan. Full of vitamins, good for you, but, it has to be admitted, unexciting to taste. In the food industry seaweed is an important source of alginates, organic substances used in an astonishing variety of ways: as an emulsifier in soups, in soft drinks, confectionery, jellies, puddings and ice-cream. It can even be transformed into the thin film used to form an edible sausage 'skin'. From the red seaweeds the chemical industry extracts agar, a gelatinous material used in bacteriological work, and vast quantities of iodine have been extracted from the brown seaweeds.

Strictly speaking, kelp is a word which applies to the burnt ash of *Laminaria* and *Saccorhiza*. In the past, a sizeable labour force, especially in northern France, was employed in burning these weeds to produce kelp for the soda which was subsequently extracted to be used in the glass-making industry. *Saccorhiza*, unlike *Laminaria*, is an annual weed, but nevertheless it grows to an astonishing length. Commonly two metres long, in one year it may stretch as much as four metres

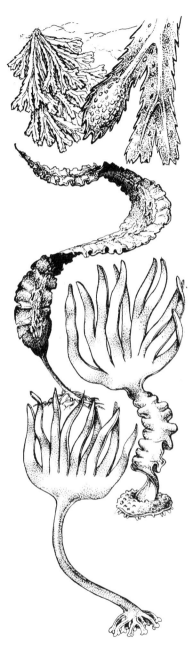

Serrated wrack *Fucus serratus*, the long frond of sugary wrack *Laminaria saccharina*, and two kelps, *Saccorhiza polyschides* and *Laminaria digitata*.

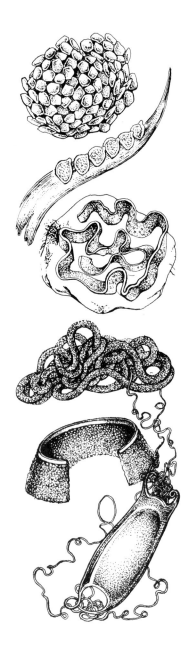

from the tips of its fingery fronds to the bulbous and warty holdfast. In spite of its great size, it is (like all the seaweeds) very flexible, able to bend with the wave action and avoid breaking. At the end of the year *Saccorhiza* dies naturally, to be cast up on the beach by winter gales, but other weeds, like the oarweed, *Laminaria digitata*, are perennial and may endure for several years unless they are much damaged by nibbling animals such as the blue-rayed limpet.

The blue-rayed limpet is a miniature snail with a translucent shell decorated with rows of brilliant blue spots, which specialises in eating into the fronds and stipes of *Laminaria*. Carving itself a shaped hollow, it spends the summer on the upper reaches of the weed, then migrates down into the holdfast in late autumn, conveniently in time to avoid the probable consequences of its own action: the weakened stipes being snapped and carried away by a storm.

Holdfasts, especially those of oarweed, are a sanctuary for many animals, and even other seaweeds. Sponges and hydroids, sea-mats, sea-squirts and crabs all congregate in the many-branched fastness, to enjoy a measure of safety from marauding predators. This is the sort of place where you are likely to find the tiny long-clawed porcelain crab, a pale and flattened creature with a belligerent pair of prize-fighter's pincers. There may be a whole collection of the eggs of different sea animals, from the flask shapes of the netted dog whelk to the cluster of sandy coloured capsules of the common whelk. The porcelain crab may even hide among the whelk capsules.

The most elegant of eggs is the *mermaid's purse*, deposited by the lesser spotted dogfish and secured to the kelp or wrack by a strong corner frond. Carefully packed into the purse is the young fish and his supply of yolk, enough to sustain his growth through an incubation period of seven or eight months, a time which allows the fish to attain an advanced state of development before it hatches. These creamy egg-purses are not difficult to find, and often enough they can be seen completely out of the water on a exceptionally low tide. This is the time to look for the 'sea hedgehog', too, the spiny sea urchin which grazes the sub-littoral rocks and weeds, moving slowly but surely on its hundreds of sucking tube-feet. Look carefully at the sides and underhangs of the low-water rocks to find one of the two species of British cowries. Closely resembling the true cowries of the tropics, but much smaller, these tiny molluscs slide over the rocks searching for sea-squirts on which to feed.

A variety of egg shapes. *Top to bottom* Cluster of common whelk, flasks of netted dog whelk, ribbon of sea-lemon, string of sea hare, collar of necklace shell and mermaid's purse of lesser spotted dogfish.

While the tide is out, the seaweeds lie down, covering the rock faces and boulders like a blanket. Though the sun and wind may dry the surface of the weed, the effect is only skin deep. Draw back the curtain and you will find that it has insulated an area which is dank and dark, a happy home for crabs and snails and even fish. Gobies and butterfish will sit out the low-water period in energy-conserving peace and quiet. Various sea urchins will be grazing.

On the face of it, the most effective way of sitting out the low water period is for an animal to find its way to a rock pool – an oasis of calm sea water – but life is not so simple, and in this wild aquarium there are problems. The sun may evaporate the surface water and concentrate the salinity. Or on a rainy day the pond will become diluted. If the pond is well supplied with seaweed then there will be a surplus of carbon dioxide at night and of oxygen by day, to say nothing of small boys with jam jars! So it is clear that a shallow pool, especially if it is on the upper shore, will be less rewarding than a deep one on the lower shore, replete with crevices and overhangs. Pool-watching is very good sport, and while the steadily increasing temperature during the day makes it uncomfortable for the fishy inhabitants, it is highly desirable to the casual snorkeller. Lying quietly on the surface, with your mask firmly in place, you have a window on another world. But do remember the one important snorkeller's rule – take a good strong breath every now and then, to give the tube a spring clean and to expel any carbon dioxide which has built up.

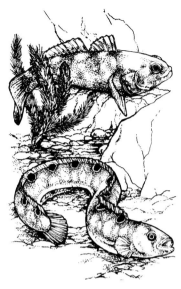

Goby (top) and butterfish.

Pools are the best place to watch sea anemones, because there they are more likely to be expanded than those left high and almost dry by the tide, when their mouth openings are firmly closed to retain moisture. The scientific name of their class is *Anthozoa*, meaning flower animals, and what an apt description this is, for the various species display an astonishing range of shapes and colours. They are relatively simple animals, with no respiratory organs, as they take in oxygen through their surface tissues. They live attached to the rocks (or, in some cases with mobile homes – on the hard shells of crabs) by a slimy disc on which the animal can move about very slowly, although most of the time it simply sits still and holds tenaciously to its anchorage. The stout muscular body column is expanded at the top to display a series of hollow tentacles circling the central mouth. The tentacles wave to entice small fish or crustaceans to within range of the stinging cells. Once

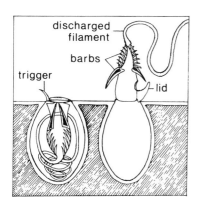

The stinging cells of a sea anemone, much enlarged.

siezed, the small creature is enfolded in the tentacles and the stinging cells (*nematocysts*) keep the prey paralysed while the anemone's digestive juices get to work. Introduce your fingertip to the waving tentacles and the physical contact will trigger the stinging cells and you will feel a stickiness on your finger ends, but that is as far as the anemone's attack will go. Before it actually starts to eat your finger it needs a chemical cue to bring the feeding mechanism into play. Since a finger is not regarded as a suitable meat course by the anemone, the cue will not be forthcoming.

Most of the anemones are sedentary creatures, more or less stuck to the home rock, but individuals of some species sometimes develop a working relationship with the hermit crab. By making its home base on the crab's shell, the anemone has the advantage of being carried effortlessly about so that it can lean over and sweep up the crumbs after the crab has finished its meal. The relationship has mutual advantage, in that the crab gains some protection from its close proximity to those stinging cells. Quite apart from the anemones, there may be tube worms and sponges and other colonisers on the hermit crab's shell. Tucked up inside with him may be a ragworm, also taking advantage of the safety and the free transport to new feeding grounds, and paying its way by aerating and cleaning up the shell interior to the crab's benefit.

The creatures which live with the hermit crab might just as easily have settled on the more conventional rock surface, and indeed the vast majority do so. One of the most striking features of a good rocky shore is the way in which every possible surface is covered with weeds and snails of one sort or another. One of the most numerous settlers is not a snail at all, although at first sight it looks like one. The acorn barnacle is a crustacean, closely related to the crabs and shrimps. Though its final phase of life is on the shore, often in such numbers that you cannot avoid walking on them (indeed they make rock clambering a good deal safer, their rough shells offering such a good grip). The animal starts its life in the fashion of the other, more conventional crustaceans, free-floating in the plankton. But when the others mature into the free-ranging life of a shrimp or lobster or crab, the barnacle comes to rest on a suitable hard surface. Though this might well be the shell of a hermit crab or the carapace of a crawfish, or Southend Pier for that matter, the most likely place is the rocky shore, somewhere in the inter-tidal area.

Once arrived, the barnacle cements itself firmly to the rock, and grows a conical shell of limey plates which interlock to protect the body and also provide a hinged *operculum* at the apex. This opening, through which the barnacle feeds, closes when the tide recedes and the animal is exposed. When the sea, with its charge of plankton food, surrounds the barnacle, it opens the trap door and six pairs of feathery legs emerge to sample the passing life, combing any food items towards the open door. You can see this happening in any rock pool, but the most effective study technique is to find a barnacle-encrusted crab and introduce it temporarily to a plastic box aquarium.

Acorn barnacles survive perfectly well on the upper shore, withstanding long periods of exposure, but in these conditions, with relatively short feeding periods, they are slow to grow. On the other hand, upper-shore barnacles tend to live perhaps half a dozen years longer than those which colonise the lower levels. The great advantage of settling on the lower shore is that the tide cycle allows longer feeding time and shorter exposure, but there is more competition for home sites. The long-term result is that lower shore barnacles cluster close together and grow tall, a form of high-rise development in which the average life span is some three years.

Many marine molluscs forage and graze over the surface rocks and boulders. Whereas those of sandy shores are mostly bivalves, those of the rocks and hard surfaces impervious to

Above left Acorn barnacles with plates closed.
Above When the tide comes in the plates react and six pairs of legs emerge to kick food particles into the interior.

burrowing are mostly single-valved, gastropod snails. Instead of burrowing down to safety, they develop strong predator-resistant shells and some, like the acorn barnacles, guard the inevitable opening with an *operculum*, a sort of trap door attached to the foot-muscle which can hold the door shut when required. The universally familiar and common dog whelks, which often live in exposed situations, are quite strong enough to be rolled about in a rough sea without being broken, but they are careful to deposit their eggs on the sheltered underside of stones and in crevices to protect them from the full fury of the sea. Clustered in these places, the mated pairs will produce two or three hundred capsules, most of them infertile and destined to serve as food for the few little snails which do emerge some four months later. Soon enough the baby snails range over the lower shore as active carnivores, searching for worms to eat. Dog whelks come in a wide range of colours, from off-white and yellow through to banded browns, and it may be that the assortment of colours which they display is related to the particular food they are taking at the time.

Dog whelks, with egg capsules.

The preferred prey of the dog whelk is the acorn barnacles which are so thickly concentrated on the rocks. In order to penetrate the limey shells they exude a poisonous secretion, *purpurin*, which relaxes the barnacle's muscles, allowing the whelk to force open the opercular plates and attack the flesh. Purpurin is a substance common to the *Muricidae* family, of which the dog whelk is a member, and which includes the spectacular tropical *murex* shells. Large numbers of these were collected in Roman times, in order to extract the yellow purpurin which, under the action of the sun, produced the purple dye used to edge the splendid toga of an Emperor. Imperial, or Tyrian, purple was also used by mediaeval monks to illuminate manuscripts.

The dog whelk, unconscious of its noble connections, has a different method for dealing with limpets as prey. Limpets are firmly attached to the rock face and have the single shell of a gastropod mollusc, far less susceptible to attack than the crustacean barnacle. The whelk climbs up on to the selected limpet and settles down to bore a neat hole through its shell, using the rasping surfaces of its belt-like tongue, a process which might take up to two days. When the long job is over, its questing proboscis enters the limpet to suck out the flesh.

Limpets are one of the commonest snails of the rocky shore. Like the barnacles, they settle on the most open surfaces, yet the two animals are not in competition. In fact, the result of the limpets' grazing is helpful to the barnacles in that it provides them with areas well-cleaned of algae on which to settle. In turn, the limpet may graze over the algae which grow on the barnacles. The limpets move off from their home base to the grazing as soon as the tide covers their rock, or even while they are still exposed to the air if the weather is wet and cool. Ranging over a metre or so, they rasp away at any fresh growth, the favoured food being newly settled seaweed spores. At high water they return home, perhaps following their own mucus trail. Home is an exact spot for each individual, because in order to avoid desiccation at low tide, the margins of the shell must make a sealed contact with the rock, in order to retain the necessary spoonful of water inside. If the rock is of a soft nature, the limpet will grind it to make an exact fit. If it is hard, then it is the shell which is ground down to conform with any irregularities.

The limpet is wonderfully adapted for its life-style. With its broad base and cone shape it is able to deflect the force of the

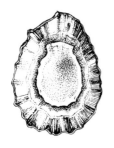

Oystercatchers have strong bills capable of dislodging limpets. They are careful to attack at the mollusc's head end (top of drawing) where the muscle attachment is least strong.

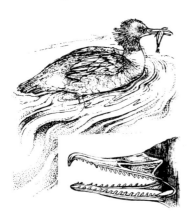

The merganser has a saw bill which is specially designed for securely gripping fish.

waves on the open shore, and its armour plating protects it from attack by most birds, provided it has enough warning for the foot muscle to get a really firm grip on the rock. One bird which can penetrate the limpet's armour is the oystercatcher, which takes advantage of the fact that there is a weak point in the snail's attachment to its own shell. If you look inside a freshly empty limpet shell, you will see a horse-shoe shaped ring, revealing where the foot muscle joined the shell. The open end represents the head cavity of the animal, and this is the end where the oystercatcher attacks, since it is least strongly held to the rock. When the shell is inhabited the head end is easy to distinguish because the cone shape is slightly lopsided, with a steeper incline at the head. The oystercatcher takes a look then makes a sideways thrust with its bill at the margin of the shell. Often enough the limpet is dislodged, to be carried off by the oystercatcher, which proceeds to chisel the meat from the shell. If the beak-blow should break the shell, the oystercatcher simply inserts its bill into the fracture and levers the snail off the surface of the rock. Empty limpet shells, rifled of their living contents, are often found on the tideline, with the tell-tale jemmy marks of the oystercatcher's beak around the margin, or the neatly drilled entry hole made by a dog whelk.

Dog whelks themselves are not immune from attack. Their shells may be found with the apex removed, the work of the shore crab, or with the shell smashed open completely by the powerful claws of an edible crab or possibly even a lobster. Larger holes in common whelks may be a clue to the work of herring gulls, especially when they are found well above the shoreline on a road or embankment where they have been dropped.

Unfortunately for the molluscs, these are not the only ways in which they are attacked. Waders, flatfish or echinoderms may swallow them whole and kill them with digestive juices, ejecting the inedible shell; starfish may force them to open; they may be dropped from a height by herring gulls. Yet they survive in uncountable numbers. Even when the tide is in, they are not left in peace by the birds. Eider ducks visit the shallow waters of northern Britain and dive not only for a beakfull of the green weeds but also to pick up small crustaceans and molluscs. Other birds, like auks and shags, dive to chase small fish over the rocky ledges. The merganser for instance, has a specially designed saw bill which is capable of gripping even a slippery customer like the butterfish. Curlews and whimbrels enjoy rooting about the exposed weedy rocks for sandhoppers and snails, while rock pipits and other small birds try their luck for flies and yet more sandhoppers in the wave-tossed weed at the edge of the water. Perhaps the most typical shore-bird is the turnstone, a wader which lives up to its name by searching and turning the weeds and stones, but the birdwatcher's favourite is the purple sandpiper, a tame and confiding little wader which dodges the waves with practised ease.

At the uppermost limits of the shore live those animals which have almost made a break with the sea and learned to become land creatures. Chitons and sea slaters, with their woodlouse-like articulated armour plates, scavenge during the night. Almost independent of the sea, they carry their eggs in a brood pouch, the young emerging in adult form without having enjoyed a larval stage as plankton animals. To gain access to the land, it is necessary for animals to be able to breathe air, to avoid desiccation, and to breed ashore without recourse to the sea. The chitons and sea slaters have gone a long way along this road, but the most fascinating demonstration of a family pioneering the route ashore is given by the periwinkles. There are four common species on the shore and each demonstrates a different stage in the process of invading the land. The common periwinkle is a very successful animal living over a wide area of the shore in large numbers. This is the creature harvested for food by winkle-pickers. Then there is the flat winkle, with its bladder-like appearance and tendency to disguise itself amongst the bladders of wrack. But the two smaller winkles of the upper shore are the ones of greatest interest in the pioneering stakes. The small periwinkle feeds mainly on lichens and is able to live high above the tideline provided it gets an occasional splash of sea water. Nonetheless, it still suffers the grave disadvantage of requiring a plankton stage for successful nurturing of its larvae.

The remaining species, the rough winkle, is an inhabitant of the upper shore, not venturing into the splash zone as adventurously as the small winkle. On the other hand it does have the all-important characteristic of being viviparous in its reproductive behaviour. The female produces live miniature snails which are independent of the open sea plankton stage and thus the species seems poised to make the final crawl up the beach to a life ashore. In fact this intertidal zone fringing the sea, so wonderfully rich in plants and animals, is a kind of transit camp, a place where creatures acclimatise themselves

The rock pipit (top) is a common shore bird all the year round, while the purple sandpiper is a welcome winter visitor.

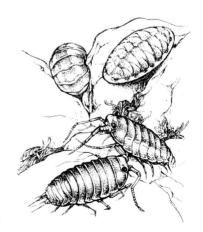

Chitons (top) and sea slaters.

for the great change from life in the sea breathing water to life on the land breathing air, at first in short tidal gulps, then for longer periods higher up the shore, till they only need the occasional splash of salt spray to keep them going. And once they can crack the problem of producing young independently of the open sea, there is nothing to stop them forsaking the influence of salt water altogether. In a few million years' time, the common and inoffensive rough periwinkle of the seashore may be making its home in our fields and gardens, having passed through an evolutionary gateway.

Duneland

The holiday brochures show sandy bays bounded by romantic rocky headlands, or long stretches of golden sand, and entice us to leave our homes for a holiday, but when we go to the seaside we demand roads and car parks, railways, hotels, promenades, ornamental gardens, and all the amenities which go to make up a resort. So in reality a lot of our sandy beaches are backed by solid concrete.

These unyielding structures which we have managed to build, against the will of the sea, act just like cliffs in many ways. They rarely give a foothold to plants and animals as the natural cliffs do, but, at vast expense, they stop the sandy beach from spreading inland and taking over. Given half a chance, usually during winter storms, the beach will try hard to move in on a slumbering town, clogging the guest house gardens with sand and strewing boulders along the promenade. This is an affront to civic dignity, of course, and sand is swept from the streets as quickly as the wind can carry it ashore.

But if the wind carries sand beyond the beach to a tract of land that Man has not claimed for promenading, then a whole new world of sand may grow up. Duneland. These duneland habitats, behind the beach, can often be recognised on the map by their local names, like Newborough Warren, Braunton Burrows, the meols of East Anglia, and the links of Scotland. Conditions have to be right – the winds, the sand, the lie of the land – but when they are, a new and characteristic landscape gradually takes shape. Offshore there may be tidal sandbanks, mysterious islands of sand which seem to rise and fall with the ebb and flow of the sea. On the foreshore there will be

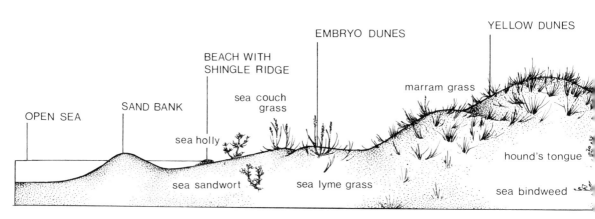

OPEN SEA

SAND BANK

BEACH WITH SHINGLE RIDGE

sea couch grass

sea holly

sea sandwort

EMBRYO DUNES

sea lyme grass

YELLOW DUNES

marram grass

hound's tongue

sea bindweed

occasional shingle banks, curious hummocks of a here-today-gone-tomorrow nature. Just above the high water mark great yellow dunes rise up, held together by tough tussocks of marram grass. Protected by these primary defences, the plant-rich old grey dunes loom up further back, and, as the climax to this succession, the dune system is backed by a marshy area of dune slacks, water which provides a happy hunting ground for birds, bugs and reptiles.

The offshore sandbanks make a safe, undisturbed place for birds to roost or hunt cockles, but clearly they are of somewhat restricted value, since they are regularly covered by the tide. For all that, they represent the nearest thing to 'home' for common seals. Unlike the grey Atlantic seal, which prefers wild and exposed sea caves and beaches, common seals tend to favour more sheltered places. They frequent sand and mud-banks in estuaries and the low island archipelagos of sea lochs. On the Wash, where a third of the British common seals live, over 6000 of them, you are most likely to see the hauled-out seals from a boat; but off Blakeney Point in Norfolk there may be fifty or sixty at a time, lying in clear view on the sandbank islands just offshore.

The seals' coats match the colour of the water, but it is always easy to distinguish the rounded shapes of their heads as they bob in the water, staring at intruders with their big round eyes. They have good eyesight, but in these muddy waters they must rely a good deal on their acute senses of smell and hearing when they search out flounders along the sea bed. There is no shortage of food for them in these waters, and the seal

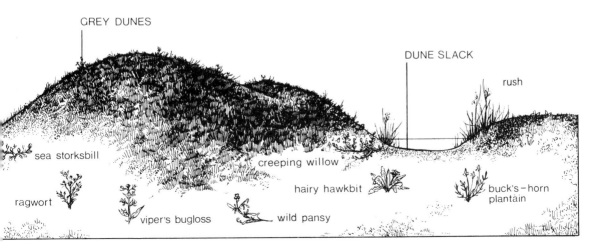

population is a healthy one, maintaining its numbers in a way that seems to have been little affected by the hunting they suffered in the past and from which they now enjoy some protection.

The seals settle on the banks as soon as the falling tide exposes some sand, then hump themselves down, keeping always within a reasonable panic-distance from the deep water. As the sandbank grows with the falling tide, so the number of seals increases, and soon the bank becomes criss-crossed with the 'tyre-tracks' left by the humping seals – you can see these tracks in the photograph below. The seals live a life half-in and half-out of the sea. They are rather slow-moving on land, but are expert divers in the water, propelled by their powerful hind-flippers.

Unlike the truly sea-going whales, the seals drop their young ashore. Whereas the grey seal pup may often spend its first few weeks passively on the beach, above high water mark and out of reach of the sea, the common seal pup must swim within hours of its birth, since it will most likely be born on a sand or mud bank which is uncovered for only part of the day.

Common seals on a sandbank in the Wash. Note the sand tracks showing the animals' progression down the bank as the tide recedes – they like to be close to the water.

The young pup will follow its mother into the sea, possibly even climbing on to her back for a short ride, then it will swim through the high water period until the sandbanks begin to uncover again. The pup will receive its highly nutritious milk feed either lying at the shallow water's edge or while it nuzzles up to its mother on the drying bank. Cow and pup will recognise each other by both smell and voice. Much of their early life together will be spent lying placidly on the great mounds of sand.

That same tidal sand, drying in the wind and sunshine, sometimes moves on, to play a part in the building of duneland. Depending on the power of the wind, you may see the sand sizzling along the beach – much paler than the firmer sand below – and stinging your bare legs and face. A strong wind is needed to get the sand on the move, and then it progresses by a kind of jumping, known as 'saltation'. When the first grains of sand are lifted (those which are easiest to carry, probably because they are smaller or drier than their neighbours) they soon fall again because of gravity. This bump down to earth jolts the surrounding grains, making it easier for the wind to lift and move them in turn. And so the process of sand moving goes on. But it is when the movement stops for some reason and the wind drops its load, that things get more interesting. The grains may be too big to move far, the wind may suddenly lose energy, but often enough it is because an obstacle blocks its path.

A major obstacle which often confronts the runaway sand is a shingle ridge, maybe part of a spit or bar, built with material brought in from another part of the coast by longshore drift. On such spits, like Blakeney Point, ridges of shingle may be thrown high up the beach, often during a storm when the power of the waves is sufficient to carry the stones beyond the reach of normal wave action. Sometimes these ridges continue to grow, so long as material eroded from elsewhere is available, to create very significant features on our coastline. When the wind blows, the ridges slow it down and sand is deposited on them, so that the process of dune-building begins. And those embryo dunes also make a home for some very attractive birds.

While the seals are able to breed on tidal sandbanks, the breeding birds must find a place completely out of reach of the sea. Even the most salt-hardened oceanic species have to do this, for example the terns, which winter off the coast of tropical Africa then come north in the summer months to take advantage of the rich fishing season around the European

Common seal. Cow and pup.

Page 76, top left Black-headed gulls colonise marram dunes in the breeding season. In winter plumage, the black cap is reduced to a spot behind the eye.
Top right The most handsome birds of duneland, a shelduck family.
Bottom Sandwich terns nest in close-packed colonies on shingle banks dangerously close to high water mark.

Terns. Little, common, arctic, sandwich and roseate.

coasts. For terns, the ideal nesting place is a sand or shingle bank, out of reach of the waves yet within easy distance of the fishing grounds. Unfortunately these are places which people find attractive, too. The little tern, for instance, tends to nest just above high water mark, exactly where holidaymakers like to tramp. Furthermore, the bird lays small eggs, in a barely recognisable scrape-nest, in widely scattered places on the shingle, not even benefiting from the protection of a noisy colony. The crowning irony is that as a species becomes rarer – and the little tern is one of our rarest breeding birds – the incentive for egg-collectors becomes greater, so it is threatened by deliberate as well as casual disturbance.

Trampling feet and breeding birds are mutually exclusive, so in many places the tern's best friend is an enlightened land owner. At Blakeney Point, for example, the teeming tern colonies benefit from the constructive management of the National Trust, not to mention the ebullient warden, Ted Eales. With the firm but friendly guidance of Mr. Eales, many thousands of people get the chance to see nesting seabirds, but at a respectful distance. The result is that everyone benefits and the terns do very well, indeed the bird list at Blakeney Point is one of the longest for any part of Britain. Projecting into the North Sea from the Norfolk coast, the point makes a good landfall for migrants, as well as being a stronghold for the tern cities. Apart from the little terns, there are about a thousand pairs of common terns and variable numbers of sandwich terns. In 1978, for instance, there were 500 pairs of sandwich terns, nesting typically close together on an embryo sand dune, almost shoulder to shoulder. This is a hazardous place to breed. The nest is no more than a saucer-shaped scoop in the sand or shingle and, quite apart from the human disturbance, blown sand or spume may bury the eggs or chicks, or an inconvenient storm may wash the whole colony away. These are natural hazards, however, and over a period of years the terns recover from them.

Other birds besides terns nest on the foreshore sand and shingle. The glossy black and white oystercatcher, or sea-pie, lives here, making an apology of a nest out of a few stones or bits of dead grass, decorated with a rabbit dropping or two. An excitable bird, the first to make its presence felt as you come round the corner, it flies around you in wide circles, peep-peeping all the time. With its long, strong, orangey-red bill, it makes a living probing in the sand for cockles and shrimps.

Sometimes several of the birds will join together for a curious performance in which they fly around in close company, then land on an undisturbed sandy place to continue an animated discussion, all of them piping at each other with as much power as they can muster.

Ringed plovers live in this kind of country, too. They are small plump birds, grey with a conspicuous black collar bordered with white. They nest in a sandy hollow, lined with a few stones or shells, maybe a bit of grass, laying about four eggs which merge into the surroundings, and which are vulnerable, like those of the little terns, to the passing feet of holidaymakers. When they are hatched, the baby plovers are sand-coloured and beautifully camouflaged. If you happen to walk too close to them, the parent bird will stage a masterly performance of feigned injury while the chicks crouch and freeze. Staggering about with a 'broken' wing, she will lure you – or another enemy like a marauding stoat or fox – to a comfortable distance away from the chicks, then take off and whistle her way through the air to rejoin her offspring.

Once established on a bare sand or shingle ridge, birds begin to alter the landscape. Their droppings enrich the vicinity of the nests. Bits of dead fish, an occasional dead chick and empty egg shells begin to accumulate. A humus develops, providing a place where plants can gain a foothold. The plants need moisture, and this, surprisingly enough, is supplied by the underlying shingle. If you move a few pebbles from the surface of the shingle, the lower ones are usually damp to the touch – and damp with fresh water. This water results from condensation, which in turn depends on the big differences in temperature between day and night. During a hot sunny day, the pebbles heat up and the air in the spaces around them expands, but with the cool of evening it contracts again and more air is sucked down into the spaces. This newly arrived air is quickly chilled by the cold pebbles and is forced to release its moisture, much as the moisture in warm breath mists up car windows on a frosty morning. Although there is never a lot of water available from this source, there is enough for well-adapted plant species to gain a hold. That is the beauty of a plant succession. Hardy pioneers become established, flourish, reproduce, decay and make way for more demanding species. The pioneer plants of the strandlines and terneries need to be tough. The salt sea is very close, so they must be able to hold on to their fresh water and to resist periodic inundation. The

Above An oystercatcher's nest is not ostentatious.
Below Ringed plovers, too, simply use a sandy hollow, lined with a few stones or shells. If the chicks are in danger, the parent feigns injury in the hope of luring the potential predator away.

succulent fleshy leaves of plants like sea sandwort show just one reaction to the problem of water storage. In the case of sea holly, the leaves have a secretion of wax on their surface to help reduce moisture loss. Other plants solve the same problem by having hairy or downy leaves, a device which traps a layer of still air close to the leaf surface, helping to reduce transpiration.

These plants attract a lot of insects, which in turn provide ready made meals for the beach birds. Under a clump of sea rocket, for instance, there will be an oasis of damp, and there the sand-hoppers will cluster. There may be flea-beetles and woodlice. All these are grist to the ringed plover's mill, and the birds will explore the sea rocket's surroundings as readily as the bumble bee will come to visit its flowers.

As a precaution against trampling, some beach plants have special protection. Sea holly is as prickly as its hedgerow namesake, and prickly saltwort lives up to its name too. Plants like silverweed and sandwort defend themselves against fierce winds and blasting sand by retreating into tight-packed rosette forms, hugging the ground, a habit which also makes passing feet less troublesome. By contrast, the flamboyant appearance of some of these pioneers in flower, like the yellow horned poppy, seems to belie the harshness of the environment.

These striving plants may annoy us by pricking our bare toes, but by providing new obstacles to the sand-laden wind and by decaying to form more humus, they make way for the next wave of plant invasion, and with it the formation of an embryo dune. The two most important invaders at this stage are both grasses, sand couch grass and lyme grass. Sand couch grass propagates readily from seed; lyme grass – which is less common – less so; but both spread most readily from specialised roots called rhizomes which can tunnel under the sand and send new shoots up through it. The tall thin leaves and feathery flowers change the aerodynamic shape of the developing dune and trap sand, but it is the rhizomes which bind and stabilise the dune, casting a three-dimensional net by way of horizontal and vertical growth. The ability of sand couch grass to spread outwards horizontally is potentially unlimited, but the plant cannot tolerate great quantities of sand piling on top of it. More than about sixty centimetres in a year will swamp it out. By contrast, lyme grass rhizomes have been shown to grow upwards 150 centimetres towards the light, and buds found sixty centimetres below the surface were still capable of growth. So the two grasses make a good team, especially as they can both survive an occasional dousing with salt water when storm waves or extra high tides invade the margins of their dune.

Sand couch and lyme grass continue the process of accretion, gradually building up the embryo dune until it reaches a height at which it is rarely inundated by the sea. Now the way is open for the kind of dune that most of us see in our mind's eye. Quite big – big enough to jump off or slide down, and sprouting all over with a greyish spikey grass – marram grass. Marram grass cannot tolerate being covered by the sea, which is why, in the natural succession, it takes over when the other species have raised the land above the level of normal sea attack. But marram has other strengths, and is a very special plant. Unlike any other, it has potentially unlimited vertical *and* horizontal growth, again by means of rhizomes. It is the vertical ability which allows dune hills to grow tall. At over thirty metres in places, the dunes at Braunton Burrows are among the highest in Britain. Marram thrives on sand burial. When a shoot is overwhelmed by sand its reaction is to produce a bud which develops into a new vertical shoot striving for the surface. When the light is reached leaves are formed and the whole process starts again, because the leaves and subsequent large feathery flowers trap yet more sand, by slowing down the wind which carries it.

The marram plant grows taller and more extensive as it builds its dune, and its outermost parts become more and more remote from the water which is stored below the sand. So it becomes increasingly important that the plant uses its available water wisely. Like the other pioneers, marram has special mechanisms for preventing water loss in this environment where the winds, whistling through the leaves, have a great potential for water removal. The stomata, small gaps in the cell wall through which water is lost during transpiration, are protected by being placed in depressions or grooves, sunk in the leaf surface. During dry weather, when conditions are especially difficult, the long leaves curl into a narrow tube to insulate the stomata from the drying outside air. The outer surface of the tube, which has no stomata, also aids water conservation by virtue of a thick cuticle. The greyish cast on a marram dune in summer is the result of all these curled leaves. The dramatic consequence of a shower of rain can often be seen as the leaves re-open, spreading a fresher green colour across the sand hills.

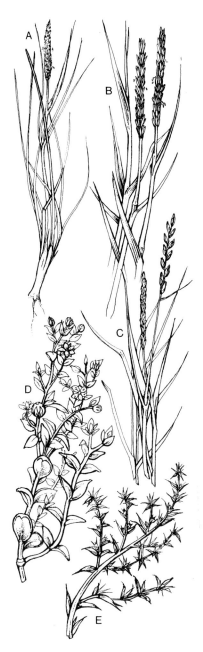

Three pioneer grasses, A marram, B lyme grass and C sand couch. The two plants below them, sea sandwort (D) and prickly saltwort (E), are at home on the driftline and among the dunes.

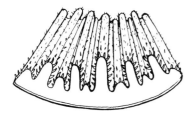

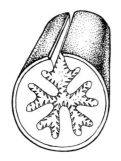

Marram grass – a remarkable plant which thrives on sand inundation. Underground shoots develop into leaves when they break the surface, to produce a typical pattern of tussocks (top). Transverse section through a leaf (centre). Stomata are located in the depressions, and become protected when the leaf rolls into a tube during dry conditions (bottom).

Marram grass will never completely clothe a dune. It grows in a pattern of tussocks made up of several groups of plants with lots of bare sand between. These open spaces give the name 'yellow dune' to this stage of the succession. On the open sand desert between the tussocks you are liable to find an unexpected number of spiders and insects. Some of these have been blown in by the wind, but some fly in by design. Hunting wasps find prey here. Tiger beetles and harvestmen wander about on the loose sand. There may be tracks and signs to see, for occasional hedgehogs and foxes, stoats and adders may pass this way. On a hot day there may be a common lizard basking in the sun.

In the yellow dunes, most living things are based on the tussocks of marram, where whole communities of animals find a home. Here the climate is much less severe. Much cooler inside on a hot day. Much damper, more sheltered. The hunting spider *Cheiracanthium* chases his prey amongst the grasses and over the sand, camouflaged by his straw colour and grey-green abdomen to merge into the sand and marram background. In summer the female builds a cocoon by binding the tops of the grass stems with silk to make a dome, which shelters her eggs. Sand dune spiders are mostly species which are also found in marshland. On the face of it this may seem odd, but the parched surface of the yellow dune is misleading, for conditions in the heart of the marram tussocks are not arid. The surface temperature will be several degrees cooler than on the bare sand, and the grass cover preserves a pocket of still air within the tussock. The result is that the interior is always humid, and sympathetic to small creatures. Several dune spiders burrow under the tussock sand to construct silken egg cells. Others have developed long, un-spider-like bodies, and spend their days clinging head downwards to a marram stem, looking as much like a piece of stem as possible in the hope of remaining unseen. At night these jumping spiders, like *Tibellus maritimus*, *Hyctia nivoyi* and *Synageles venator*, roam the stems and sand, searching out small insects on which to pounce. One of them, *Attulus saltator*, is only found on sand dunes, whereas the others are equally at home, along with a greater variety of species, in wetland marshes. Also at night, the caterpillar of the shore wainscot moth, *Leucania litoralis*, will emerge to feed exclusively on marram spikes. During the day it lies hidden in the sand. There are snails in the dunes, too, and it is worth searching the vegetation for them, especially after a good shower of rain.

Black-headed gulls may colonise marram dunes and transform them into a noisy and sociable clubland. Whereas the other gulls tend to prefer more rocky homes, on open cliffs and island clifftops, these settle for dunes, saltings, and boggy moorland pools or freshwater lakes. Marram dunes suit them well, and they build their nests, close together, on the low vegetation between the tussocks and on the tussocks themselves. A scruffy affair, the nest is woven from whatever material lies close to hand and is sufficient to provide a saucer for the three eggs. Both parents take turns to incubate and then to feed the chicks, which soon become infected by the general air of excitement and wander about from tussock to tussock, genially buffeting and being buffeted. Genial most of the time, that is, for like most gulls, the black-heads will take advantage of any opportunity, and that includes a neighbour's fat chick. It may also include any plover or tern chicks which offer themselves, so black-headed gulls are not entirely welcomed by the tern-conscious nature reserve warden. A gull colony may cover a considerable area of sand dune, and over a period of time the trampling and droppings will affect the vegetation. Certainly, once the yellow dunes are established, the gulls help to pave the way for the next wave of plant succession on the sheltered side, away from the immediate effects of salt spray and blowing wind.

Blown sand is the key to life for marram grass. Each layer of sand deposited on the plant stimulates it to produce fresh, vigorous shoots. But as the dune grows backwards from the sea, so the supply of sand diminishes, and the marram loses its grip, making way for a lively newcomer, sand sedge. Sand sedge thrusts up green leaves with military precision, from a horizontal rhizome which penetrates the sand in a dead straight line. And on ground enriched with rabbit and hare droppings, wind-blown tideline debris, fragments of shell, and so on, mosses and lichens also establish themselves. Houndstongue, storksbill and sea bindweed and a host of other plants continue the work of stabilising the landward face of the dune system. Over a period of hundreds of years the 'grey' dune develops; the greyness largely due to the abundant growth of lichens. Well-drained, firm and dry, this is the dune country the walker enjoys.

It is in the grey dunes that the rabbits are very much at home. The well-packed sand is ideal for burrowing and the dune grasses make ideal grazing, indeed the rabbits' feeding

Some dune spiders have long, un-spider-like bodies, resembling the marram stems, in the hope of remaining unseen.

Skylark.

Caterpillars of the cinnabar moth eating the leaves of ragwort.

preferences determine the nature of the plant cover here, since they readily devour clovers and erect grasses but leave the ground-hugging dwarf plant forms alone. Quite apart from the droppings, which are scattered everywhere, the presence of rabbits is unmistakably shown by the typically short-cropped grass in the vicinity of the burrow entrances. They dislike getting their belly fur wet in the long grass and prefer to be near the burrow in case of emergencies. The disturbed sand around the burrow entrance is often a sympathetic holding-ground for ragwort, which does well here because rabbits are not keen to eat it. On the other hand, ragwort is the preferred food for the caterpillars of the cinnabar moth, and if you find them at all, they are likely to be present in large numbers.

Grey dunes are skylark country, too. A walk across the springy turf is almost always accompanied by the liquid warbling of that stout brown shape, climbing effortlessly high into the sky to proclaim ownership of the dunescape, before sinking down to the ground. Meadow pipits nest in these parts too, but their song-flights are much less musical. Looking rather similar to the skylark, they are easily told apart by their habit of sitting tight on a marram tussock, peeping plaintively if the nest is nearby.

A complete dune system may stretch back a considerable distance from the sea and this means that the valleys between successive dune ridges, known as 'slacks', are more or less insulated from wind and sea, especially the slacks between the oldest 'grey' dunes. Here the constant deposition of animal and vegetable humus allows the sand to hold more water. In the grey dune slacks fresh water may be very close to the surface, allowing plants of damp pasture land, like hairy hawkbit and buck's-horn plantain, to flourish. Sometimes, especially in winter, the water may even lie on the surface of the slack, forming pools of fresh or brackish water.

This system of dry dunes and wet slacks suits the shelduck, the most spectacular bird of the grey dunes, very well. A large duck, almost gooselike, it has a white body enriched with a chestnut chest band, dark green head, red bill and pink legs. The shelduck likes to nest in the well-drained dunes, often turfing a rabbit out of its burrow to establish a home underground. Once the ducklings – and there may be a good dozen of them – are hatched, the whole family must make its way to shallow brackish water or an estuary to feed. In the dune system, the damp slacks and pools are ideal.

No dune walker's day is complete without a scramble down the side of the dune into the damp world of the slack. Here the creeping willow flourishes, a miniature forest of yellowish stems growing a foot or so from the ground. The name comes from the way the root stock creeps along just below the surface, its plentiful decaying leaves providing rich humus, helping other plants to establish themselves in this near-bog; plants like the masses of meadow buttercup, purple orchid and lady's smock. In the miniature lakes, pink water speedwell, edible watercress and water crowfoot hold sway, while rushes hold fast at the edge.

Smooth newts may be found in these ponds and, if the temperature is right, the tadpoles of a rare amphibian, the natterjack toad. Confined to a very few, well-protected localities, and suffering because of the insatiable demand people have for sandy heathland as a habitat for coastal development, the natterjack has to fight hard to survive. It has special living requirements, always a disadvantage nowadays, when the most successful animal species tend to be those with the most catholic and opportunistic tastes. Natterjacks need sandy soil in which to burrow and warm ponds in which to breed. Dune slacks are ideal.

Natterjacks are quite different from the common toad. Smaller and less warty, they have shorter hind legs – made for walking, not jumping. Grey green, with a striking yellow stripe running right down the middle of the back, their skin is less dry than in the common toad and with their greater secretion of mucus they are adapted to survive greater heat, a decided advantage in the dunes. They can dig well with their fore-limbs, throwing sand out behind them and they are good climbers. Nocturnal by nature, they will nevertheless show themselves at the burrow entrance often enough, and may well be seen at any time of the day. At hibernation time they easily dig down a half a metre into the sand, where temperature and humidity conditions are more stable, but in early summer they migrate to the dune-ponds, where they lay long strings of eggs, several thousand of them, where the water is shallow. Sadly, this often dries out at the most inconvenient time, providing yet more food for the birds.

Short-eared owls are typical of duneland and, unlike the other owls, they are diurnal. With their long wings they glide and wheel over the dunes, searching for voles. So one way and another, a lot of plants and animals find a living here. Yet it is a

Some colourful plants of the damp dune 'slacks'. A lady's smock, B meadow buttercup, C purple orchid, D creeping willow, E sea milkwort.

community that can have its life rudely shattered overnight. A dune, especially a yellow one, is a precarious sand castle, even when covered by a diverse and well-established flora.

The binding skin of dune vegetation can easily be broken. Rabbits may burrow and nibble too assiduously or people may enjoy themselves too energetically. Sliding down the steep windward face of a yellow dune is undoubtedly great fun, but it may mean that next time you arrive for a holiday the dune has disappeared. The wind will be quick to grasp the opportunity offered by even the slightest chink in the dune's defence and a small bare patch where the vegetation has been scarred can soon enlarge into a full-scale blow-out. Big blow-outs, sitting like huge bowls among the sand-hills, signal the potential instability of the system. This instability is something we should respect, because sand dunes really matter, not only to the shelducks and lizards and natterjack toads but to the people who live and work behind the beach. Paradoxically, these fragile systems play a vital role in our coastal defences. Natural protectors, they allow the influence of the sea – the spray, the sea-warmed air, and the maritime species – to penetrate inland, but keep the sea itself at bay.

If dunes are to build sound sea defences, they need plenty of building material – sand – but in some parts of England, the east coast for example, this is in short supply, as the prevailing winds are offshore, allowing dune-building only in limited periods. The inadequacy of the dunes, coupled with the gradual sinking of the land as the relative sea level rises, is one reason why the low coasts of Norfolk are so subject to flood and erosion. Once the dune line has been breached, the sea can spread far and wide over the flat lands behind. This is what happened so disastrously in 1953, when a storm surge in the North Sea caused flooding from Yorkshire to Kent, submerging about 800 square kilometres of country. Near Lowestoft, for example, the soft cliffs were cut back nearly ten metres. Ten metres during one storm! This shows only too clearly the power of the sea, and the archives of East coast towns are filled with lists of houses, churches and even whole towns which foundered when the sea took the upper hand.

Sometimes the natural dune defences must be breached on purpose, as happened during the last war, when sluices were opened on land at Minsmere, in Suffolk, as an anti-invasion measure. But whether the dunes are breached by Man or by nature, the resulting dune lagoons are a paradise for birds. In these shallow brackish waters which have a connection, however tenuous, with the sea, enormous quantities of fish fry and insect larvae develop. Waders and ducks move in for the feast. This is where the shelduck families come to search for small crustaceans and molluscs. On the nursery shallows and mudflats they trample, scoop and scythe vast numbers of small creatures for food.

At Minsmere, the Royal Society for the Protection of Birds has carried lagoon management to a fine art. Over a period of some twenty years they have created an environment where a thousand pairs of birds breed, and you may see fifty different species in one day. By controlling the water levels and providing carefully engineered 'scrape' islands, they have improved living conditions for such breeding visitors as avocets and terns. Bearded reedlings, marsh harriers and bitterns breed there, all species which have suffered drastically from habitat loss elsewhere in the country. From carefully sited hides at Minsmere the visitor may enjoy the richest birdwatching in Britain, but the real triumph is the demonstration of what can

From the well-designed hides at the RSPB's famous bird reserve at Minsmere in Suffolk, visitors enjoy close views of waders and sea-birds like sandwich terns.

be done to the fauna and flora of a place by thoughtful intervention. Minsmere and its marvellous riches are the happy result of a lot of hard work and controlled flooding. But a mature dune system, with its hinterland of brackish lagoons, is also ripe for 'development' of a different kind. Although it represents a superb example of natural succession, rich with highly adapted plants and animals, it is a relatively simple process nowadays to reclaim it, transforming duneland into barley fields or conifer plantations. We hope to have shown that it is worthy of a better fate, and deserves its rightful place in Britain's coastal heritage.

Muddy waters

Page 91 An aerial view of Newtown estuary, Isle of Wight.

Estuaries are places where rivers finally reach the sea: the Thames, Tamar, Humber, Severn, Mersey, Firth of Forth, for example – all familiar names because of their connection with great sea ports. On a map, estuaries look like an inland arm of the sea, but on the ground it is sometimes difficult to believe that they are part of the seaside at all, looking more like a brimming lake or some extra-terrestrial landscape of shimmering mud at different stages of the tide.

Estuaries have their origin far from the roar of the sea waves. On their journey to the sea the rivers change from raging upland torrents, through swift-flowing streams to broad, majestic reaches. Always the flow is downward to the sea. At the end of the journey, when the river finally discharges its load of water and sediment into the ocean, there is a region where water of different origins mingles, to flow up and down the lower valley with the rhythm of the tides. The water may be of full sea-water concentration when the tide is flooding in, whereas during low water periods the water which remains may be nearly fresh – the outflow of the river. Between these two extremes, the sea and fresh waters are mixed together, but not uniformly so. Salt water is denser and heavier than fresh, so the fresh river water may form a layer above the incoming salt of the sea. Of course some mixing does take place, and one of the effects of this is to further stimulate the deposition of silt. By a process known as 'flocculation' suspended sediments are attracted to each other and, clumping together, they grow bigger until they fall. The tidal mud banks begin to grow.

In the majority of British estuaries, like the Tamar, for example, which we have known and loved the longest, the large-scale deposition of silt began with the end of the last glaciation. Before the Pleistocene Ice Age the Tamar had formed its valley, running 100 kilometres to the sea in Plymouth Sound, but when the ice was formed vast quantities of water were stored, frozen, upon the land, so that the sea-level dropped by as much as 60 metres. Because the gradient from the land to the sea was now so much steeper, the rivers flowed faster and with greater energy, so that deep gorge-like valleys were excavated. When the ice melted, the sea-level rose again all round the country, allowing the salt water to return and drown the over-deepened river mouths. Known as 'rias', these drowned valleys form the most common type of estuary.

The return of the sea meant that the rivers slowed down again and as a result they were forced to drop more and more

sediment at their mouths. So much sediment, in fact, that the rias became filled with material won from the land. The great depths of this mud, over thirty metres on the Tamar for example, are often revealed by test borings for engineering works like power-stations. The sea-level is still rising and sedimentation continues, ensuring that in geological time estuaries are destined to be very short-lived phenomena. All the processes of deposition are striving to raise the shimmering mud to the status of dry land.

On an estuary, more than any other part of the coast, it is possible to see these processes of deposition at work. Stay, best of all on a boat, for a day and watch the tide ebb and flood; stay for a fortnight and see the change from neap to spring tides. Best of all, stay for a year to experience the highest equinoctial tides flooding the landscape and their lowest counterparts revealing channel beds which see the sun only twice a year.

In the dynamic habitat of the estuary, plants play a star role. By helping to trap silt they form and shape the very land upon which they grow, like the sand dune species which help to build their own homes. Again, like the dune flora, the plants form a succession, from the pioneers which struggle in the most difficult conditions to the well-established and often long-lived plants which grow where the marsh merges almost imperceptibly with the land. The full range of habitats which produces the succession can be seen best when the tide is out. Then the water which remains (mostly fresh water which flows continuously from the river) will flow past bare, unvegetated mud-banks. In the six-hourly cycle of the tide, these banks will be exposed to the sunlight for only a short period at the end of the ebb and the beginning of the flood – not long enough for the survival of plants, which, containing chlorophyll, need the sun to power them.

As more mud accumulates, the surface of the tidal bank will reach a threshold at which there is just enough light, for long enough on every tide, to allow plants to grow. After *Enteromorpha*, the bright green slimy looking plant which requires submersion and cannot tolerate much exposure, the first two important plant colonists are glasswort, or marsh samphire, and cord grass. The latter has taken over in many estuaries, but glasswort, a fleshy bright green plant which looks like a miniature tree, most effectively demonstrates the way in which the plants prepare the way for a drastic change in the environment.

Unlike most of the salt-marsh species, glasswort is an annual, and the success of its little seedlings depends on the force of the tide. A strong tidal current will dislodge the shallow-rooted plants, and this same swiftness of current may stir up the sediment to such an extent that light cannot penetrate the water effectively and again the plant cannot grow. If the plant does overcome these obstacles, it will slow down the flow of water around and over it and force sediment to settle. By thus trapping the mud, the bright green forests of glasswort gradually raise the level of the mud surface until it is exposed for longer periods on every tide. As much as three centimetres a year may be accreted, the rate being greatest in autumn when the glasswort has reached its greatest size. Indeed autumn is the time when all salt-marsh species are most efficient as silt traps.

The first plants to grow on the bare mud make a big impact on the landscape when the tide is out, although of course they cannot be seen when the flooding tide covers them. After this pioneer stage the most striking aspect of the plant community is the zonation, where different plant species grow in bands, or zones, according to the length of time they are submerged on every tide. An estuary with a big tidal range will support a marsh with broad, well-displayed zones – say a pure glasswort community, followed by glasswort in association with seablite or sea manna grass, giving way to carpets of thrift and sea lavender, with pasture grasses like sheep's fescue at the highest levels of the marsh, where tidal inundation is least frequent. On a small range estuary where the difference in level between high and low water is not great, the zones are likely to be compressed and confused, with particular species adapting to their position on the marsh by changing their growth form. Sea aster, for example, with its purple flowers so reminiscent of Michaelmas daisies, may be a tall straggling plant two or three feet high in places where it is flooded to that depth; or it may flourish as a stockier little plant in the higher levels of the marsh where inundation is not a big problem.

In reality the location of particular species is often determined by the micro-habitats of the marsh; the creeks and pools and fresh-water drainage channels which add so much to the variety of a salt-marsh, especially when seen from the air. Drainage channels on the bare mud usually take their chosen course because of slight irregularities of the surface, and once established tend to persist when the mud is colonised by plants. The flooding tide rises first up the creek beds which, being at a

Page 94 Huge flocks of waders visit British estuaries either to stay for the winter or for refuelling stops on migration. This photograph shows knot on the Cheshire Dee.

Fescue grass often forms a close turf on the estuary saltmarsh.

Sea purslane, a shrubby perennial with grey-green leaves which favours the well-drained sides of tidal creeks.

lower level than the plant-covered marsh provide the first points of entry for the rising waters. The depth of the creeks which criss-cross a salt-marsh varies a great deal, but as the water which flows in them is always deeper than the water which floods the marsh itself, the flow is faster. This relatively swift flow of water favours erosion of the channel, rather than deposition of sediments, and so the creek system is perpetuated.

In this rather unstable region of the creeks, plants must adapt. Algae which manage to grow on the steep creek banks, like *Vaucheria thuretti* for example, develop a good grip on the mud by means of a gelatinous secretion. Creeks are rather bare of plant life because of the erosion that goes on, but the plant most characteristic of the creek banks is the shrub-like sea purslane, which colonises both sides of creeks, often meeting to form a bridge over the narrower channels. Sea purslane demands good drainage at root level, so the slightly raised creek banks suit it very well and its pale grey-green foliage, winding like a road through the marsh, is a clue to the whereabouts of creeks, which all too easily cut off the unwary marsh-walker.

As the tide rises, the creeks form waterways, carrying water-borne seeds and root fragments into the upper marsh. Cord grass often becomes established in this way. Capable of reproduction from seed and from root fragments, it has such an amazing ability to accrete silt that, once it has a foothold, its vigorous growth may completely block a drainage channel. Once this happens, the way is paved for the formation of salt pans, often seen as circular depressions, where the plant species are different from their neighbours on the surrounding marsh.

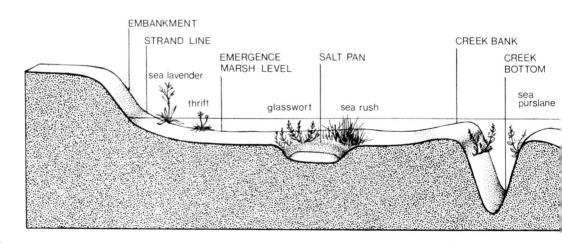

The salt pans begin to develop when the water of a spring tide, which covers the whole marsh and its carpet of plants, finds that its retreat is blocked by the growth of a sturdy clump of cord grass, or any other plant for that matter. The water therefore remains, becoming more and more saline as evaporation gets to work. This water may become so saline that the blocked creek section remains totally bare of plant life, like an open pond. More usually it is invaded by plants which are normally found in the pioneer zone, like the salt-tolerant glasswort or seablite, or cord grass itself may expand to fill the entire area. These salt pans, where limiting factors like salinity and temperature become intensified can be compared with the rock pools of the open coast.

Because they are at a lower level than the surrounding marsh, the salt pans trap and retain water with each tidal inundation, so perpetuating the super-saline conditions. It is only when the plants have grown big and vigorous enough to trap a lot more silt that the pan may eventually be elevated to the level of the surrounding vegetation. The species most able to achieve this growth is again the ubiquitous cord grass, indeed it is the super-plant of the estuary in the late twentieth century. First found in Southampton Water in the 1870s, it has spread rapidly in both directions along the south coast, and is now the major colonist, often forming neatly circular islands as it invades the bare mud. This hybrid grass is accelerating the natural process of reclamation, raising the land surface until it is almost unaffected by the tide. Man can achieve this rapidly by building dykes to keep out the flooding tide, and in Britain as

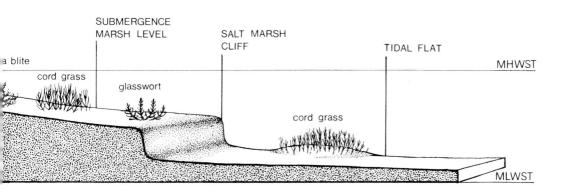

97

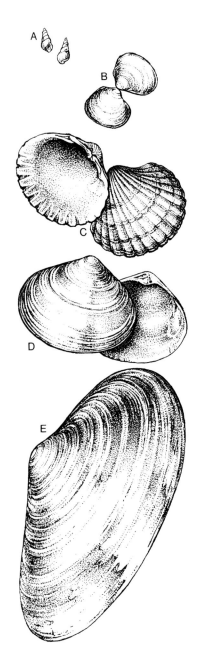

Common molluscs of the estuary.
A *Hydrobia*, B *Macoma* (Baltic tellin),
C *Cardium* (common cockle),
D *Scrobicularia* (peppery furrow),
E *Mya* (sand gaper).

early as Roman times, Man was trying to increase the area of the land – notably around the Wash – by these means.

The plants which colonise the mud at the edges of the estuary must be capable of sustaining life at all stages of the tide and throughout the seasons. This same rule applies to the resident animals like the molluscs and crustaceans which, during hot summers with lots of evaporation or winters with lots of rain, must be able to cope with the great changes in salinity and still maintain a constant concentration of salts in their bodies. The common shore crab, for instance, with which we are all familiar on the open sea shore, is able to thrive high up the estuaries where a good deal of its time is spent in near-freshwater conditions. When the surrounding water becomes diluted, it is able to regulate the situation by increasing the saltiness of its own blood.

The shrimps, worms and shellfish which live on and under and at the edge of the mud have a similar tolerance of a wide salinity range. Like their relations on the sea coast, they also take advantage of an ability to burrow down or hide under stones, which provide a more sympathetic environment. Cockles may be found wherever there is sand or gravelly mud, in enormous numbers. Other shellfish which live just out of sight also thrive; on the Tamar estuary, for example, scientists have measured the Baltic tellin's numbers and say there can be nearly six thousand in a square metre of mud. Since they inhabit the top ten centimetres, the mind boggles at the thought of their concentration. Not surprisingly, they form a major food source which is enthusiastically exploited by both birds and fish. Other shells, like the peppery furrow and the sand gaper, burrow deeper down and use long siphons with which to gather their surface food. Yet for all their concealment, they are not immune from attack by birds.

The smallest of all the estuary sea-shells, however, lives a good part of its life exposed on the surface of the mud. *Hydrobia* is just six millimetres long, the size of a grain of wheat, yet because of its great abundance it, too, is an important source of food for waders and ducks. Crawling over the mud, it feeds on bacteria. We once dropped a concrete mooring-clump into the mud, only to find it swarming with *Hydrobia* shells just a few hours later, obviously enjoying the bacterial film which had already begun to grow on the freshly made concrete surface.

There may be over a thousand ragworms in a square metre of mud, living in individual burrows lined with slime and emerging to feed when the incoming tide covers them. Look closely at the mud surface and you will see their tell-tale tracks in the mud, radiating from a central hole. As much as ten centimetres long, they have a conspicuous red blood vessel running the length of their backs. Many bait-digging anglers will testify to their possession of chitinous jaws which can give enough of a nip to hurt a finger, even if they do not draw blood. Reaching out of the burrow, they scavenge the mud around them and also take small crustaceans which pass by. Opposum shrimps must be a likely prey. They dart about in the shallows in large numbers at low water and on the rising tide, filter-feeding on the minute plankton plants. Another crustacean, the sandhopper *Corophium* hauls itself out of its burrow with hooked antennae and scavenges the water-covered surface. It, too, is hunted by fish and birds. So although there are relatively few invertebrate animal species living in the demanding conditions of an estuary, they exist in astounding populations and support large numbers of visiting hunters, fish, bird and mammal.

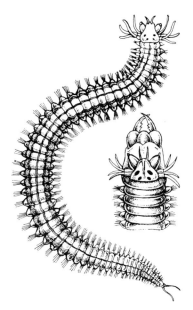

Ragworm *Nereis*, with close-up of chitinous jaws.

Flounders are typical estuary fish, though they are the only flat fish to be found there. Spawning at sea, they are nevertheless able to tolerate fresh water for long periods. Hunting over the shallow mud as the tide comes in, they take cockles and tellins, shore crabs and shrimps and gobies. Grey mullet, toothless browsers, swim up on the tide to graze the seaweeds. In the autumn they will patronise yacht marinas, sucking the fringe of green weeds which sprout richly around the waterlines of boats – especially those which are rarely used. The mullet may, on occasion, take an animal larva or a small shrimp, and it is also partial to a morsel of bread – even the mass-produced variety – which makes it a fairly easy catch for the fisherman.

Grey mullet graze algae and often lie motionless at the surface, basking in the sun.

Eels are very common in estuaries, spending some time there during the uphill journey to the river from the Atlantic of their youth, and also on their last, downhill, journey in the silver livery of spawning. The Atlantic salmon are passage migrants, too, although their life-history is almost the exact opposite of that of the eel. Most of their adult life is spent at sea, growing fat on the rich food of the Arctic; but they return to their native rivers to spawn. In a summer of drought, they may congregate in the estuaries in large numbers, waiting for the rainfall which provides them with enough fresh water to smell their way up the rivers. This is the time when they may be taken in seine nets, and thereby denied the chance to spawn or fertilise. Never miss a chance to join the netsmen at their work and perhaps see one of these splendid fish. Look carefully at its body and, if it is fresh-run, there may be a number of sea-lice clinging to it. These parasites do not survive long in fresh water, so the estuary is the most likely place for you to see them. Only a centimetre or so long, they have a hollow flattened body which acts as a suction disc, pressing against the fish skin. Two prehensile claws dig into the flesh and grip hard.

Fresh-run salmon often carry sea-lice (inset).

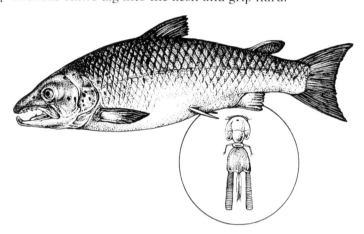

All these fish represent a food source for man, and they are accordingly netted, trapped and angled. They are also assiduously hunted by birds. The salmon's main enemy is certainly Man, as his size makes him an unlikely prey for most birds. We have watched ospreys hunting salmon in the tidal creeks of the West Country in August and September, when they stop over for a few weeks on their journey from the breeding season in Scandinavia, to the wintering grounds in Spain. However, their main prey at this time seems to be mullet, which, because they spend a lot of time at the surface, make an easy catch for the fish-hawk. The osprey is a leisurely hunter, flying up and down a calm reach a few times before it decides which individual fish to swoop down and pounce on.

Eels are taken in fair numbers by the cormorants which spend the greater part of the year living in these tidal waters. Choosing a likely area, the bird does a jack-knife dive into the rich muddy water and searches the bottom, to emerge, maybe a minute or two later, with a wriggling eel as long as himself. The struggle to swallow it may be dramatic and prolonged. Cormorants will take flounders, and these flatfish are also

Page 101, top Ospreys visit estuaries to sample the sea fish while on migration in spring and autumn. *Bottom* Salmon netsmen at work.

diligently stalked by herons. Grey herons, along with cormorants and shelducks, are typical estuary birds. Indeed, while cormorants go down to the sea for the breeding season and shelducks leave for a few months while they moult their flight feathers, the heron is the only one to stay faithful to the creeks and mudflats throughout the year.

The heron is a sociable bird whilst nesting at the heronry, and at roosting times, but is a somewhat solitary hunter. Each individual has a feeding area which he regards as his own, and he patrols the water's edge as the turning tide brings the fish fry and fat flounders within his reach. While he may spend a good deal of time standing at the water's edge, relaxed, with half an eye open, or standing with outstretched neck, leaning forward to wait for the fish to come to him, his most successful fishing by far is accomplished when he stalks actively. Wading very slowly through the shallow water he watches, and then stabs. Small fish are swallowed whole, on the spot. Larger ones are carried off to the nearest field or to the saltings, shaken and broken, then eaten at leisure. As the tide rises over the mudflats, the heron will fly majestically to join his mates, perhaps in a convenient waterside tree, or perhaps standing in a group in the middle of an undisturbed field, to preen and rest.

While cormorants and herons fish, shelducks hunt over the exposed wet mud on the ebb, as well as in the very shallow water at the edge of the tide, looking for molluscs and shrimps. Paddling across the mud, they sweep the surface with their bills, searching out the *Hydrobia* and tellins. They may also indulge in the 'puddling' which is so typical of gulls on wet sandy beaches or flooded playing fields. Puddling up and down with their broad webbed feet compacts the mud or sand, and forces both shellfish and worms to the surface.

In springtime and early summer the estuary is a fairly quiet place from the birdwatcher's point of view, because the tidal nature of the habitat means that very few birds breed there. Mute swans may build their nests on the salt-marsh, a risky thing to do, since the nests and eggs are often swept away by spring tides. Plenty of small birds may colonise the reedbeds where they can build out of reach of the tide; and there may be a few non-breeding redshanks or curlews or plovers. But at this time the vast majority of the estuary birds are thousands of miles away in the high Arctic and in Scandinavia, so it is specially good to have the company of the shelducks, which do stay to breed. They will have been courting noisily since the

Curlew, calling in flight.

turn of the year; anything up to a dozen birds promenading on the mud and taking part in highly formalised dancing parties. Long before spring they have chosen a nesting-place, perhaps underground in a rabbit burrow, or hidden in the depths of a bramble bush above the marsh, and while one bird sits tight on the dozen eggs, the other will stand sentinel out on the saltings or on the fields nearby.

When the ducklings hatch, after thirty days of incubation, they must go down to the mudflats where they find their food. At twenty-four hours of age, they are led from the burrow by their parents, across fields, ditches, hedges, roads and all – maybe as much as four miles, though usually much less, and across the saltings to gain the safety of the mud. Inevitably, on the way, some ducklings fall prey to marauding foxes and crows. Once on the mud, the duck introduces them to the delights of ragworms and shellfish, while the drake stands guard. Gulls and crows are always ready to take advantage of an unwary duckling which strays too far from the safety of the family circle, and by the time the ducklings are a week or two old, the brood is usually reduced to half a dozen or less. Shelducks have a very loose family bond. Week-old ducklings will readily join the nearest brood or crèche when they are alarmed, and by the time they are three weeks old, they are almost independent. From now on they will mix freely with the ducklings of other families, forming a crèche with anything up to a hundred members supervised by just one pair of adults. Whether these playschool supervisors are self-appointed, chosen, or just landed with the job by virtue of being the last pair to hatch ducklings, is unclear. Certainly by the time ducklings are a month old, their parents are beginning to leave the home estuary to fly away on a moult-migration, usually to the Heligoland Bight. They join many thousands of others to find safety in numbers during this vulnerable period, when they are confined by their flightless state to sandbank and sea, while they moult and grow new flight-feathers. In the early winter they make a leisurely way home.

While the young shelducks are perfecting their hunting in mud and shallow water, the young herons are fishing the water's edge on the rising tides, pecking at floating feathers and bits of wood, as often as at a passing goby. By midsummer, the first of the returning waders begin to appear: some to re-fuel and pass on, perhaps to West Africa, and some to stay for the winter.

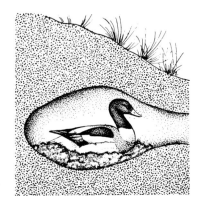

Shelduck in nest burrow.

On the Tamar we expect to see our first godwits, still in their splendid breeding plumage, by about the middle of July. And by the middle of August there are thousands of waders, though the peak may not be reached till nearer Christmas. Waders are the birds which make estuaries such exciting places for birdwatchers, yet at first sight many of them seem almost dowdy in plumage, out of the breeding season. Their sheer numbers can be impressive, though. In Britain their mid-winter population will reach nearly a million and a half. Sometimes a shimmering mudflat will be alive with their busy bodies, advancing across the rich feeding ground like a terrible army, decimating the worms and shellfish in their path. They migrate over vast distances, from the fly-rich Arctic breeding grounds to the worm- and mollusc-rich mudflats and lagoons of northern Europe and Africa. Small to middling in size, they are gregarious and open-living characters, richly varied in their adaptations to their prey. They are master aviators, found anywhere in the world where there is a shallow patch of wet.

Waders find food by touch, taste and movement, looking for tell-tale signs and probing with bills which have a mass of sensory nerve endings. Their bills come in an astonishing variety of shapes, and the beauty of it all is that a whole host of different species can live off the same tidal mudflat because to a large extent they are hunting at different times, different levels and in subtly different habitats. While the fish and the cormorants stay in the water, the herons and black-headed gulls and some of the waders are at the water's edge, while many others spread out over the exposed mud. Dunlin, for instance, the most numerous of all, prefer wet mud, especially close to the waterline. Twisting and turning in aerial flocks, they bomb in to peck for sandhoppers and *Hydrobia*, worms and small tellins. Clouds of knots fly in from the high Arctic, alternately darkening the sky and then flashing brightly as they manoeuvre on the wing. On the mud they pack together tightly in such numbers that it comes as no surprise to find that there are over a quarter of a million of them wintering in Britain.

Redshanks, one of the common companions of any estuary day, with their noisy 'tew' calls and their white wing-bar, are in competition with the others for worms and sandhoppers, but they have a preference for tidal pools and the water's edge. With a brisk walk and an occasional dash, they peck, jab and 'mow' the surface. It has been calculated that a redshank may peck up to 40,000 times a day in pursuit of a full stomach. The much

Left and below Dunlin on the mud-flats. The dark belly is typical of breeding plumage. They prefer wet mud as a hunting ground.
Bottom When the tide covers the feeding grounds, waders congregate to roost. Redshanks and curlews.

Wintering ducks (male and female) on the estuary. *Top to bottom* Mallard, wigeon and teal.

less common greenshank also likes to chase shrimps and small fry in tidal pools, whilst the godwits, black-tailed and bar-tailed, choose to work slowly and methodically over the open mud, heads down and bills busy, feeling the texture of the mud and extracting tellins and worms. With their longer bill they can reach down into the mud for the larger shells, ten centimetres under the surface.

The curlews are everyone's favourite, with their long down-curved bills and that lovely liquid cry. Solitary, or in parties of mixed company, they stand out by virtue of their size, as largest of the waders. Strolling over the mud, they pause to probe, then maybe run several metres to pick up an unwary ragworm. With a beak reach of some fifteen centimetres they have free choice of all the mud creatures, even reaching down to the peppery furrow shell. While they may not quite reach down to the lugworms in the bottom of their chambers, they can and do catch them by the tail as they reach up to expel detritus in the worm cast. Cockles and other shellfish are swallowed whole, the indigestible shells subsequently rejected in the form of a pellet. On the upper shore, especially in autumn, they hunt the abundant shore crabs by sight, rather than by touch and taste.

Other birds visit the estuary in spring and autumn as passage migrants, like the osprey we have already mentioned. The odd spoonbill may show up for a few weeks or even stay the winter. Terns, which may have bred on the south and east coast or in the inland marshes of central Europe, come to fish for a few weeks before passing on to congregate in the Irish Sea, the Wash or the Moray Firth.

Swans, ducks and geese which may have bred thousands of miles to the north and east, migrate to enjoy Britain's milder winter weather. The harder the weather, the further south they penetrate. So whereas in a mild winter the West Country may see only mute swans, a harsh winter in the north will soon present us with an influx of Bewicks and whoopers as well. Many thousands of wild ducks arrive to patronise the saltings, where they find winter supplies of seeds, carried down by the rivers and deposited on the salt-marsh at high water. The abundant seeds of sea purslane and other marsh plants are also welcome. Mallards, wigeon and teal are the commonest.

Geese are birds of the saltings, too. They may fly inland to graze the barley fields, but they return to the wide open marshes to find safety for roosting. In Scotland and the northern half of England, while the whitefronts come in thousands, the greylags and pinkfeet come in tens of thousands. The most maritime is the brent goose, which feeds on the low water beds of eel-grass in the lower estuary, although it will also graze the green seaweeds and take the occasional mollusc or shrimp.

Apart from the birds, a fair number of mammals visit the estuary from time to time. Foxes, rabbits and grey squirrels hunt and graze the saltings; otters fish and mink haunt the tide-banks looking for anything that moves. Grey seals chase salmon and common seals chase flounders. If conditions are favourable, allowing peace and quiet, the seals may lie out on a low water mud bank or an isolated rock many miles from the sea and wait for the returning flood. However, when small whales venture high into the narrowing creeks they run the risk of being stranded. Porpoises are often seen in the estuary waters, perhaps chasing mackerel shoals. Bottle-nosed dolphins and killer whales may venture into the muddy waters, too, looking for salmon, so these 'barren' wastes turn out to be important feeding grounds for a long list of hunters.

Estuaries are wild, sometimes alien and forbidding places, but they have a richness of life and a constantly changing pattern of light and texture that creates a strong attachment for those who come to love them. The tidal and seasonal comings and going of birds in wheeling flocks, serve always to underline the importance of the mud and salt-marsh as providers of food. Because, to the uninitiated, they seem such worthless places, they face continuous assault by Man. The mud and salt-marsh acres seem fated to exploitation by water barrage or drainage engineers, and those who seek to build oil, airport and dock

Wintering wild geese. *Top to bottom* Greylag, pinkfooted, whitefronted, brent. Brent geese feed on estuary eel-grass, while the others fly inland at night to forage in fields.

installations. This ecosystem, one of the most naturally fertile in the world, combining nutrients from both land and sea, is highly vulnerable to the terrible power wielded by Man, the arch-despoiler. The fragile green shoots of glasswort may pioneer a mighty salt-marsh, but they cannot resist the 'improver' without a bit of help.

Islands

Islands have instant appeal. They may only be pieces of land surrounded by water, but they have an interest and value out of all proportion to their physical size. Thousands of them exist, yet new ones are constantly being formed. A new island gives cause for rejoicing, whether it is a brand new world thrust hissing and bubbling through the sea by a volcano, giving Man a chance to extend his territorial waters and stake new claims; a sheer rock at last separated from its parent cliff; or an ephemeral island, appearing only when the tide drops, to provide a convenient resting place for our coastal birds or seals.

Seven or eight thousand years ago Britain became an island. Not a dramatic event, it took place gradually over a period of thousands of years, during the waning of the last Ice Age, long enough for plants and animals and people to make decisions about which side of the water they were going to live. During the Ice Age, great continental ice-sheets clothed the land. All that frozen water, locked up on the land, had come from the ocean and had the direct effect of lowering the level of the sea in relation to the land. But the Ice Age was not uniformly cold. There were warmer interludes, when glaciers began to melt, returning some water to the sea. Then there were colder periods again with more ice, so the sea level went up and down in sympathy. Eventually, the shift to a warmer and wetter climate became more permanent. The ice, which had clothed the whole of Britain north of a line drawn roughly between the Severn and the Thames, began to melt, bringing the sea and its influence higher on to the land, until finally the last of the dry land, where ships now sail the Straits of Dover, was submerged. That probably happened about 5500 B.C.

We became an island race because the rising sea cut us off from the rest of Europe. But there are other ways of island-building, and they are going on all the time around the shores of Britain. Take, for example, the formation of mud banks, which is particularly common in the south-east of England. This comes about because the sea level is still rising – about one millimetre a year is the current estimate. The rise in level means that rivers flow more sluggishly, because they are gradually being robbed of their downhill gradient to the sea. Slower waters have less energy to carry their burdens of mud and silt, so they drop them, to form mudbanks which gradually increase in size and height until they achieve the status of dry land.

Another kind of low-lying island, close to the shore, can be formed when off-shore sand and shingle banks grow sufficiently

Approximate land mass

WESTERN LIMIT OF ICE

SOUTHERN LIMIT OF ICE

Land-bridge with
continent of Europe

Page 112. top Midland and Skomer islands from the mainland.
Bottom left Rabbits benefit from the shortage of predators on islands.
Bottom right Bluebells and sea campion brighten the cliff slopes of Skomer in early Summer.

This page. top Lesser black-backed gull at nest.
Bottom The razorbill's egg is pear-shaped to reduce the risk of its falling off the ledge.

to raise their heads above the waves at all states of the tide. Walney Island, famous for its breeding birds, probably came about in this way, and in January 1972 the British Isles increased their number by yet one more, when a new island appeared off the Isle of Wight, a mile north-west of the Needles. As the Coastguards explained to *The Times*, 'There has been a shingle bank there for years, but it must have built up, and is now three or four feet out of the water'.

The famous Needles of the Isle of Wight are islands themselves, of course, but were formed in a very different way. They were the result of erosion – chips off the old block. The erosive power of sea waves seeks out weaknesses in the cliffs and exploits them relentlessly. Given time, a crack becomes a chasm, and in yet more time the sea may rush through. The jointing pattern in the chalk at the western end of the Isle of Wight has thus determined the existence of the islands or 'stacks' of the Needles. Many islands which lie close to the shore are formed in this way. Favourite resting places for birds, they give an extra dimension to the coastline. They are the result of differential erosion, and above all other factors it is their geology which ordained that they would become islands.

The Needles, island 'stacks' formed by erosion in the near-vertically jointed chalk of the Isle of Wight.

The powerful appeal of islands is easy to understand, whether it is to own one, to live on one, or merely to visit one to camp, play, and pretend to be pirates. People are fascinated by islands and often give them a notoriety out of all proportion to their size. Small islands tend to be inhabited by recluses, scientists, eccentrics and poets, but if they are big enough, they grow to support specialised versions of mainland society. The isles of Scilly, the Isle of Wight and the Isle of Man are good examples. On an island, the human communities are different from those of the mainland. Their problems, such as communications, building sites and shelter, have always forced them to be so. And it is the same for the plants and animals. So while many things on an island may be the same as the mainland – the rock, the soil, the climate – the factor which makes all the difference is the separation.

Skomer, off the southern horn of St. Bride's Bay, is separated from the Pembrokeshire coast by a mere thousand yards. The main mass of the island, 722 acres of it, is made of strong igneous rock, resisting for the most part the attack of the sea. In some places however, where softer sedimentary rocks meet the sea, the result of their weakness can be seen. The 'Neck' is the best place to look, for here the sea to the north and south of the

Page 114 A puffin returns to the nest with a beakful of sand eels for its chick.

island is divided in one place by only eleven metres of land – a defence which is being gradually whittled away by a sea intent on forming yet another new island. In this way Middleholm was cut off from Skomer, and the forces which managed to do this can well be imagined by watching Jack Sound when the tide is running.

With a westerly gale to help it, the flooding tide may drive a furious seven knot current, forcing a maelstrom of white water through the narrow gap between Middleholm and the mainland. And the even narrower gap between Middleholm and Skomer is hardly less wild. The eddies and overfalls caused by numerous isolated rocks confuse the scene and the violent tide-race strikes awe into the heart of any sailor-man. Yet, in reasonable weather and with local knowledge, the Sounds are navigable and the passage to Skomer is a peaceful and pleasurable half-hour trip. In the summer months the boat will make its way across a sea alive with puffins and guillemots, razorbills and fulmars. Long before the wide-open arms of North Haven welcome you to the island itself, you are warming to the magic of the place. Steep cliffs guard a central plateau, a tableland some sixty metres above sea level, and the whole land mass is a natural sanctuary for wild creatures, including people, protected from the fierce competition of the mainland. There is security here, where seabirds may nest safe from attack by mainland predators like foxes and stoats. The climate is mild, with less rain than in other parts of West Wales, and whilst the weather may be changeable, gales and rainstorms are usually mercifully brief, and frost is almost unknown.

Skomer has been inhabited for a long time. Although there is no documentary evidence pre-dating the Norman occupation, there is plenty of visible proof that people have lived there since at least the Iron Age. Below the rocky outcrops leading to the Mewstone are the clear outlines of field enclosures, with the hut sites and circles of a community which lived over 2000 years ago. Those long-dead farmers must have found it worthwhile to brave the crossing, and there is no reason to suppose that they lived anything but a full life. With plenty of rich grazing for goats, cattle and sheep, they occupied an island that was easy to defend and lacked the wolves and beasts of prey which must have been common on the mainland. In addition to their domestic stock, they enjoyed a summer influx of seabirds which must have improved their standards enormously. It has been calculated that they could have had

On treeless islands, crows may build in bramble bushes.

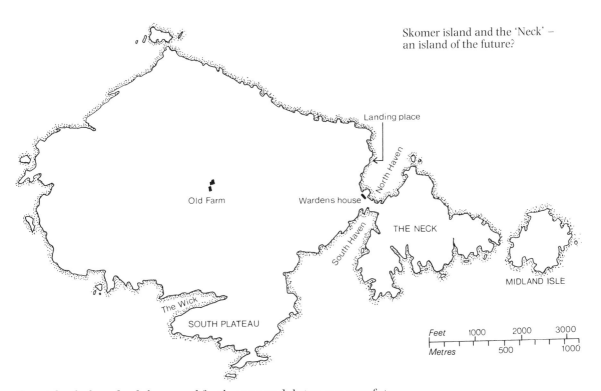

Skomer island and the 'Neck' – an island of the future?

Landing place

North Haven

Old Farm

Wardens house

South Haven

THE NECK

MIDLAND ISLE

The Wick

SOUTH PLATEAU

Feet 1000 2000 3000

Metres 500 1000

the pick of a hundred thousand fresh eggs and, later, 70 000 fat young birds – representing some twenty-five tons of edible meat. With fresh meat in summer and dried in winter, they need have suffered no shortage, though doubtless they complained of a monotonous diet!

Today the island, owned by the Nature Conservancy Council and managed by the West Wales Naturalists' Trust, is inhabited only in summer. The warden and his family live there, visited by working scientists and large numbers of day trippers anxious to sample the richness of the wildlife. Although conditions are by no means luxurious, at least the scientists have the benefit of a well-built timber house, something which the early settlers would have found very difficult to construct, for one of the significant omissions from the island's plant list is trees. There are precious few of them, finding what shelter they can from the salt-laden Atlantic gales. Yet even in the absence of trees, tree-nesting predators like buzzards and crows maintain a healthy presence. Forsaking their natural preferences, the buzzards build nest mounds in sheltered rock crevices overlooking the sea, and the crows make do with what they can find, nesting in bramble clumps, and old field walls.

Buzzard at nest in cliff crevice.

Thrift, the universal seaside plant, equally at home on cliff-top turf, saltmarsh or stable shingle. Well able to change its shape to suit the environment, the plant may grow in flattened rosette form on exposed cliffs (or mountain tops where it also flourishes!), or develop thick cushions of luxuriant leaves where the climate is kinder.

Skomer makes up for its lack of trees with a rich carpet of other plants. There is, after all, a diversity of habitats here, from the freshwater lake in the centre of the high plateau, through acres of good grazing and gentle slopes to the steep cliffs at the sea's edge. Landing on the island in June, your first impression is of a vast carpet of red, white and blue, where the strong colour of red campion, and the white flowers of sea campion growing thickly on the cliff slopes, contrast with the fast-fading bluebells. And as you plod up the grassy cliff path, it becomes clear that the bluebells are associated with the most extensive plant of all – bracken. In the face of the cool Atlantic winds its crozier shoots are slow to unfold, but as the days go by, it dominates the island flora. The lesser celandines and ground ivy which live cheek by jowl with the bracken will already have flowered and seeded in the spring sunshine. Other plants benefit from the developing bracken – wood sage, Yorkshire fog and the fescue grasses all do well in the damp shady area under its umbrella. But the bluebell is the plant which benefits most of all from its presence. Close to its protector, the blooms are thickest. Normally a woodland plant, it enjoys the moisture conserved by the sun-sheltering fronds of bracken.

Bracken cannot survive in the face of the severe winds and on the thin soil of the exposed south-west part of the island. In these areas, the most spectacular plant show is provided by cushion-beds of thrift, which grows so extensively in some parts that you have no choice but to walk on it and enjoy the spring it puts in your step. On a warm day it makes one of the more memorable resting-places of anyone's life!

Away from the sea-campion and thrift slopes, the plants in the most exposed areas exhibit the classic outcome of selective suppression by wind and grazing. Both influences produce similar effects, favouring the growth of dwarf forms which hug the surface of the ground, hardly showing their faces. But the most powerful influence of all is that of the rabbits, which impose a rigorous grazing test on any plant which wants to survive. From the casual visitor's point of view, the close cropped springy pasture is one of the delights of the island, but a superabundance of rabbits certainly results in a less luxurious plant cover. Rather in the way that one of the few garden lawn plants which can survive repeated close shaves with a lawnmower is the dandelion, so the rabbit infested areas on Skomer are characterised by hardy ground-hugging, rosette plants.

The rabbits are constant companions on any walk over the island turf. With no foxes or stoats to spoil their enjoyment (or any other predatory mammals for that matter), their only enemies are the buzzards and great black-backed gulls, and rabbit numbers are presumably controlled mainly by the available vegetation. They thrive, and have done so except for recent attacks of myxomatosis, since Norman times. We know, for instance, that in 1324, when the island formed part of the estate of the Earl of Pembroke, that while the total pasturage was valued at £2.75, the return from rabbit trapping was estimated at £14.25. The rabbits represented a profitable crop, harvested each winter by resident ferreters. In the summer, when the grass was at its best, sheep and cattle were ferried to the island for fattening, and the seabirds were cropped for eggs and fat young. This was the farming pattern through six centuries. A great deal of work on improving walls and enclosing fields made the island farm at one time a prosperous place, exporting cattle, sheep and pigs, and especially the seed corn for which coastal Pembrokeshire was always famous. The once-splendid farmhouse was built sometime around 1700, but now remains only as a forlorn shell, adjoining a row of sheds used as summer accommodation by visiting students and itinerant film crews.

One of the many attractions of islands is that they provide homes for unique animals, which can only survive away from the rough-and-tumble of competition on the mainland. As living proof of the effects of ecological isolation, we have the Orkney vole, the Scilly shrew, the Skokholm mouse, and so on. Skomer is famous for its vole, an island race of the familiar bank vole, and it also has a field mouse of distinction. Although neither of these animals is a separate species in the strict scientific sense, since each can breed with its mainland cousins to produce fertile young, they nevertheless have distinctive features resulting from their adaptation to island life. Both are significantly larger than their mainland cousins, and this feature is true of the small mammal populations of many islands. Bigger is better, certainly in the case of a fight, but it's not entirely clear why island mammals should acquire this characteristic. Perhaps the absence of ground predators has something to do with it.

The Skomer vole is a very attractive creature to meet, and it lives in its favoured bracken habitat in great numbers, thicker on the ground than mainland voles. Apart from being bigger, it

The effect of island isolation. The bigger and redder Skomer vole (bottom) is an island race of the mainland bank vole.

is redder in colour, but the most noticeable difference, once you have one in your hand, is the easy-going character of the animal. It is very tame, and inclined to sit up in your palm and gaze into your eyes with a benign expression far removed from the fast escape reactions of a mainland vole.

How did the Skomer vole arrive on the island? There are two theories. One is that it was already established there, a very long time ago, before the sea made Skomer an island. Another is that it was introduced accidentally by way of the agricultural to-and-fro, at some time since the original Iron Age occupation. This second version seems the most likely. Work on island sub-species elsewhere has shown that the physical characteristics of an animal race may undergo evolutionary change in a surprisingly short span of time in conditions of isolation. But the exact nature of the survival value of redness, largeness and tameness is not so easily explained.

It is a great deal easier to see the attraction of Skomer to birds, since an island is in many ways the answer to a seabird's prayer. For a good part of the year the sea-going birds have no need of land at all, but for the vital purpose of breeding they must come ashore, since they have not yet found a way of incubating eggs on a seaborne nest. The attractions of Skomer are obvious enough – plenty of nest sites, little disturbance and no ground predators. As a result it is one of the best bird islands in Britain, with a breeding population of many thousands.

Not all the visitors to Skomer are ocean-going species. The coastal gulls which spend their days scavenging for offal around the Milford Haven fish docks, roost there at night and nest there in the summer season. Commuters like these have many influences on the island life. Probably it was a gull which first introduced the myxomatosis virus to the island, by way of a carrier-flea from a mainland rabbit. And often enough a suspicious growth of garden weeds or farm cereals owes its origin to seeds carried in by gulls and deposited in their pellets.

On the gentle slopes of the plateau there are colonies of lesser black-backed gulls. Not so long ago their eggs were collected in great numbers to be sent to the grand hotels in London as delicacies, and during the war they represented a welcome resource to egg-starved Pembrokeshire. Their nests are everywhere, untidily built on the ground amongst the bracken, each at a comfortable distance from their neighbours, but forming part of a highly sociable community. In the central part of the colony the ground is so battered and trampled by their courtship displays and their coming and going, that even the thrusting bracken is beaten back.

The relationship between the birds and the vegetation is very close. Quite apart from the effect of trampling, the enrichment of the ground by nitrogen-rich droppings – guano – encourages a healthy growth of red campion, for instance. The attractive pink flowers of this plant are characteristic of the herring gull and lesser black-back breeding areas, places where there is not too much wind-blown salt spray to contend with. Fortunately for campion, it is not much liked by rabbits, which only eat it if they must, and, so long as there is no drought, the plant does well, fed by the bird droppings. Guano greatly enriches the soil, adding phosphates, potash and lime, as well as the nitrogen already mentioned. Add to this the odds and ends of food discarded by the gulls, and the inevitable collection of feathers and eggshells, dead chicks and bits of seaweed, and one way or another the gulls bring a varied collection of things to influence and select the island flora. Only when birds nest in close company, as in a gannetry for instance, does the enrichment and trampling become so intense that all vegetation is eliminated.

At one time there were hundreds of great black-backed gulls on the island, but there is no doubt that these large and highly successful predators were having a detrimental effect on the populations of those species which Man, in his wisdom, considers more interesting and welcome. And, since the increase in the gull population is itself a result of Man's influence (an increase in the availability of food in sewage farms, tips and fish quays) it has seemed a proper function of island management to control their numbers. As a result of much effort on the part of the warden, the population on Skomer is now maintained at about thirty pairs.

The impressive great black-backs tend to nest on prominent rocky outcrops on the higher ground, perhaps overlooking the sort of gentle bracken slope favoured by lesser black-backs. While the sitting bird incubates the giant eggs, the off-duty bird enjoys a panoramic view from a nearby promontory. When the chicks hatch they tend to stay close to home, provided they are not disturbed, until at a couple of months old they are able to fly independently of their parents. By this time the vicinity of the nest is littered with evidence of past meals – rabbit legs and fish bones – along with regurgitated pellets. This is the sort of place where you'll see the sad remains of puffins and Manx

Gulls. Greater and lesser black-backed, herring and kittiwake.

Manx shearwaters visit their island nests under cover of darkness, running the gauntlet of gulls which, given the chance, pick them clean, leaving only the tell-tale breast-bone and wings.

shearwaters which have suffered the fate of sacrifice to the gull family. In the recent past, one of the common sights on Skomer was the remains of shearwaters – two wings and a breast-bone picked clean – but one of the happy results of the gull control has been that the shearwater numbers have increased and there are now fewer corpses littering the island.

If you weren't in on the secret you would have no idea that on Skomer there are a hundred thousand pairs of Manx shearwaters nesting underneath your feet. There is no day-time sign of them, apart from the burrow entrances which you might reasonably assume belong to rabbits. Silently occupying their underground homes during the day, they wait for the dark of night to venture out into the open. Although it is superbly at home in flight or on the sea, the shearwater is very much at a disadvantage on land. Because its webbed feet are placed well back on its frame, it waddles about in a rather clumsy fashion, half-helping itself with its wings and disappearing into the safety of the nest chamber with an almost audible sigh of relief. Each pair of birds incubates the eggs on a 'week-on, week-off' shift system, and during its time off, the off-duty bird makes a remarkable journey of six or seven hundred miles to the Bay of Biscay for its staple diet of sardines. On its return, in company with thousands of others, it waits out at sea for darkness to fall, before it risks flying in to the dangers of the island terraces.

One of the magical experiences of Skomer is to stay up late on a dark night in June, listening for the first cautious cackling of the underground shearwaters as they wait for the relief party to appear. Round about midnight, the air begins to fill with the sound of demonic squawking, like a thousand cockerels cut off in their prime, and a torch beam cast upwards catches the occasional glimpse of a soot and whitewash body flashing past. Masters of the air, they crash land and, grounded, become a half-helpless struggling mess of wings, body and legs. Walking along any of the grassy paths at night you must watch your step, for there are bemused shearwaters everywhere. Bemused they may seem, but they are successful enough as a species. The sky is full of them, and on a good evening, the sea holds a giant raft of many thousands more.

When daylight comes, there is no sign of a live shearwater to be seen. Only the burrow entrances gape open as evidence that there is life underground. And, of course, as well as the shearwaters and rabbits, there are puffins living a subterranean life as well. The thrift-dominated slopes at the cliff-tops are the chosen site for the puffin villages. Here and there, benefiting from the newly dug soil enriched with guano, patches of stinging nettle and ragwort mark the burrow entrances. And, down below, only just out of sight, the baby puffin fattens on a rich diet of sand eels.

During the day there is not much activity at the nest area, but towards evening the puffins gather in rafts close inshore, taking off to perform spectacular flights round and round the bay before plummeting in to land near the burrow. Carrying a full beakload of sand eels, they pose and enjoy the evening air a while before disappearing below ground. We are always puzzled over the way they manage to catch and carry so many fish, for the gaily-coloured parrot beak may grasp a row of a dozen at a time. It is obvious enough why they need so many. Sand eels may be solid goodness, but they are on the small side, and a baby puffin must be demanding. It seems that the slight serrations on the upper mandible of the beak operate in close conjunction with the mobile tongue. The bird dives underwater and hunts in the sand eel shoal. Picking off its first fish, it grips the head firmly between the back of the tongue and the mandible. From now on, subsequent fish are packed from the back, as the tongue progressively bends up and grips head after head, until the beak has a full load caught in a vice grip. Then it's back to the nest, a row of sad little tails drooping from either side of the beak.

The congregation of brightly coloured puffins decorating the cliff banks is one of the main attractions of Skomer. With their short narrow wings and rapid-beating, fast flight, they whirr about the inshore waters with the carefree air of clockwork toys. While the puffins prefer the gentle cliff slopes, the other two common auks, the razorbills and guillemots, choose the crevices and ledges of the sheer cliff faces, sometimes in enormous numbers. Along with the kittiwake gulls which cluster thickly along the faults, shakes and bedding planes of the vertical cliffs, they form the seabird cities which have such an overwhelming impact on the visitor.

Sea-going birds which, again, are at a disadvantage on land, the auks confine their activities ashore to the immediate vicinity of the nest, flying in with webbed feet outstretched as air-brakes in a delicate stalling manoeuvre. Guillemots are the most numerous. Standing upright, penguin fashion, almost shoulder to shoulder on any suitable ledge, they have a slender pointed bill, a smooth chocolate-brown head and upperparts.

Puffins have serrations in the roof of their mandibles, making it possible for them to carry up to a dozen slippery sand eels.

Razorbill coming in to land, its wings and webbed feet acting as air brakes.

Top Kittiwakes and guillemots.
Above Gannets, greeting display.
Right Auks, like these razorbills,
spend much time in sociable 'rafts'
on the sea.

Incubating a single pear-shaped egg, which is carefully designed not to roll off the ledge if disturbed, they find safety in numbers and a common cause. All members of the colony tend to lay their eggs at the same time, so the birds act almost with a single purpose, sticking close together in order to fight off predators and to benefit from group strength. The chicks huddle together on their precarious ledge, never walking more than a few token inches. Then the day comes when they all take off and leave the ledge for the first solo flight, gliding down to the safety of the all-embracing sea. The few birds left behind are likely to be snatched up by the constantly watchful gulls, ravens and jackdaws, an example of natural selection in action.

Razorbills, with their deeper, thinner bills, are black where guillemots are brown, and although they nest nearby, they tend to have slightly different site preferences. Where the guillemots nest shoulder to shoulder on the exposed ledges, the razorbills are more inclined to hide themselves under boulders, or to half-hide in crevices and corners. They may go for holes in scree-slopes or group themselves amongst boulders. Nonetheless, if the country suits them, they may be present in fair numbers. Like that of the guillemot, the nest consists more of a site than a construction, but there may be a few token pieces of vegetation, or a couple of stones alongside the egg. Being less thick on the ground, razorbills suffer more from the attentions of gulls, but they seem able to fend off the jackdaws.

The seemingly endless toll of auks taken by oil pollution makes it hard to believe the scientists' contention that auk populations remain at a fairly stable level. There is no doubt that in the twentieth century we are seeing a diminution of their numbers at the southern end of the breeding range, in the bottom half of the UK. One of the distressing results of the auks' predilection for leisurely migration, spending a great deal of time socialising on the water as they travel from the western Mediterranean to the northern breeding places, is that they tend to swim into oil slicks. The result is inevitable, as with clogged feathers and oil-burned lungs they die in large numbers. They also succumb to the increased number of gulls, and it may be that they are affected by changes in fish distribution associated with the general temperature rise of our twentieth-century sea. In the south of Britain, many old-established puffin colonies are now gone forever, while the guillemots and razorbills just hold on by their beaks to ancestral breeding sites in the Isles of Scilly and the West Country.

Three common island-nesting auks. *Top to bottom* Razorbill, guillemot, and puffin.

Fulmar at the nest site.

Happily, most of the birds you can see on Skomer are doing well, even increasing in numbers. Twenty years or so ago, when one of us first visited the island, fulmars were just beginning to breed. Now there are over 200 pairs, and the sight of those thick-necked soarers with the straight wings riding the cliff thermals is now a common but still joyful experience. And, though they don't nest on Skomer itself, the gannets, the most spectacular of all north Atlantic seabirds, can be seen every day through the breeding season, because on the neighbouring island of Grassholm, only a few miles to the west, there is a thriving gannetry. When we flew over Grassholm in a light aircraft in early June 1978, the whole of the northern half of the island was white with the sitting birds, 20 000 of them. At the breeding place, gannets build their nest mounds at a carefully calculated beak-striking distance from each other. In the face of constant trampling and a powerful rain of guano, no vegetation can survive and the whole area is a sea of white, at least from a distance. Close to, the gold-capped heads, vicious beaks and forward-looking blue eyes, set on top of a large white body are a striking sight. Twenty thousand of them makes an overwhelming spectacle – a true seabird city.

Away from the breeding island, gannets make a living as plunge divers, hurtling down from the sky to chase mackerel or pilchards, cushioning the force of the impact with a padded breast. Yet although they are truly at home at sea, gannets, like petrels, kittiwakes and auks, can survive only with the sort of breeding safety afforded by an island, the most rewarding of all natural habitats.

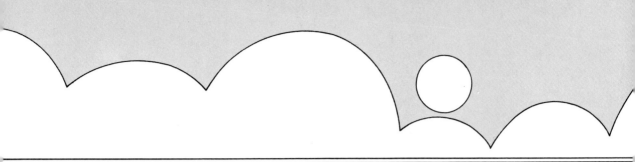

The strandline

Messing about in boats is certainly one of life's great pleasures, and patrolling the strandline of a wide-open sandy bay is another. The waves which transport sand grains to build the beach also deposit a motley collection of floating junk and treasure. Bits of weed, wood and all sorts of clues to the profuse life of the sea find themselves cast up by the tide. As the time of high water passes and the water recedes, a strand of debris trails along the golden sand and records the high water mark for all to see. Spring tides will amass the debris high up the beach, while subsequent, lesser, tides leave a sequence of lesser strandlines progressing down the beach like contour lines. Storm tides will wash the slate clean and leave it shining and blank ready for the next message to be drawn.

Exploring these strandlines evokes an excitement akin to that of seeing the trawler catch cascade on to the deck when the net's cod end is released. The light of day will reveal a string of biological treasures, or maybe, a disappointing array of tatty weed and broken fish boxes. But there is always hope; on a beach walk you might find anything from an empty limpet shell to a crate of oranges!

Most typically the strandline will consist of a pile of seaweed fronds and stipes, torn from a nearby rocky shore by wave action. Look carefully and the weed will probably be colonised by hydroids and nibbled by molluscs. There may be the egg cases of whelks, rudely deprived of their chance to deposit their larvae into the plankton. The fresh weed itself, if there is enough of it, may attract the local gardeners or farmers, who collect it as a fertiliser. (It is said that four women and one man, aided and abetted by a panniered ass, are able to collect six to eight tons in a six-hour day.) Other creatures besides people are glad to see an influx of weed with all its rich feeding possibilities. Pushed to the very top of the beach by the action of the sea, it slowly rots down to a warm glutinous mass. Underneath it the scavenging sandhoppers find a sympathetic home, emerging at night to crawl or leap about. Lift a pile of rotting weed and the air will sing as they rise in clouds. These sand fleas, like the winkles, are well on the way to becoming land animals, with their eggs carried in a brood pouch and the young independent of the plankton stage.

There are fully paid-up land animals which also inhabit the seaweed piles, such as beetles, flesh-flies and small oligochaete worms. The kelp fly feeds on the decomposing weed, and may be present in enormous numbers. Its eggs, each with a built-in

Kelp-flies on decomposing weed.

air bubble to help the embryo fly survive the occasional high-water inundation, are laid in the wrack, and subsequently the emerging larvae help in the process of weed decomposition.

With this wealth of insect and crustacean food, it is no surprise that, in walking the tideline, you will find you are not the only beachcomber. While it is true that foxes and hedgehogs come here to forage, you are unlikely to see them in broad daylight, but many passerine land birds come to chase flies and beach fleas and their larvae. Robins and sparrows, pied wagtails and starlings all enjoy rich pickings from the weed, in company with shore-birds like rock pipits, purple sandpipers and turnstones. These shore-birds are remarkably well camouflaged, and since they are also rather confiding, unpanicky creatures, you may almost stumble on top of them before they fly off. Even then they are likely to cover only a short distance before they land again, in a small party perhaps, to work over the debris in search of titbits.

September gales and winter storms blow great quantities of weed ashore. Sometimes, if they are violent enough, they may litter the shore with tellins or cockles. Sea mice, too, may be deposited in vast numbers. This slug-shaped creature, up to ten centimetres long, is in fact a worm; the largest of the British polychaetes, and it is worth examining carefully for the pleasure of seeing its iridescent hairy coat. There may also be empty cases of tube worms to be admired for the mastery of their construction.

After a storm, farmers collect large quantities of mineral-rich seaweed for fertilising their fields.

Sea-mouse *Aphrodite aculeata*.

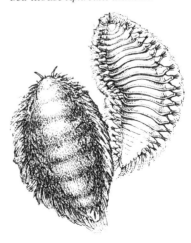

Successive tides tend to concentrate the broken or abandoned shells of marine molluscs into colourful strandlines of their own. There is perhaps the chance of finding a cowrie shell, and almost certainly there will be a galaxy of painted and whorled colours and shapes of other sea shells. Various empty egg-cases will litter the beach. Spongy masses the size of a tennis ball – the egg capsules of the common whelk – are common finds. After the tiny snails have emerged from the soapy fluid of the capsules, the ball loses its grip on the weed or stones to which it was attached, and gets cast ashore. Or it may still be firmly attached to a stipe or holdfast of some weed which, in turn, has been torn away and thrown to join the beach debris. Looking like pieces of damp sponge, they are said to have been used by sailormen as a form of soap for cleaning their hands. We have tried this, and regard them as a poor substitute.

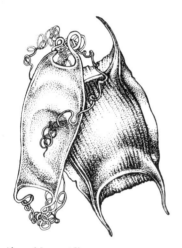

Above Mermaid's purses – the horny egg-cases of dogfish and skate.
Above right Mass of egg capsules deposited by the common whelk.

Mermaid's purses are common strandline objects. The horny egg-cases of dogfish, skates and rays, they are usually empty by the time they find their way on to the beach, and a tell-tale slit in the capsule betrays the door through which the young fish launched itself into the sea. Dogfish eggs have an off-white milky colour to them, and are easily identified by the long curly tendrils which extend from each of the four corners, possibly still attached to a bit of the weed which formed an anchorage during incubation. The black purses of skates and rays have stiffer, shorter processes at the corners, since they were attached to stones or weed by a sticky part of the main capsule. As in the dogfish, though, the 'horns' have an important function, since they are hollow and allow a current

Right The tiny valves of the
shipworm *Teredo* act like a drill bit,
leaving a log (or an unprotected
ship) riddled with tunnels.
Below 'By-the-wind sailor' *Vellela*,
stranded ashore.
Below right The violet sea snail,
supported at the surface of the sea
by its raft of bubbles.

of water to pass to the interior of the capsule, carrying oxygen to the embryo.

Sea potato tests often arrive on the shore, but they are so fragile that they soon get broken up to become part of the beach material. Even a gentle breeze may blow them over the sand. Pick one up carefully if you want to see the symmetrical rows of tube-foot holes in the grooves of the upper surface.

The egg masses of the cuttlefish may sometimes be found on the shore as bunches of small 'grapes'. They may be separated from or still attached to their seaweed anchorage. The adult cuttlefish lives amongst the shallow-water eel grass forests on sandy bottoms, hunting shrimps which it gathers with fast-flung sucker tentacles. Rather surprisingly, the cuttlefish is a mollusc, though certainly a complex form, and its shell – the 'bone' – is one of the common strandline finds. In the live animal this cuttlefish 'bone' is a hydrostatic organ which acts as a buoyancy regulator. The porous, cellular structure acts as a gas tank with a partial vacuum facility which makes it possible for the animal to pump water in and out of the buoyancy tank in order to adjust for pressure changes according to operating depth, in more or less the same way as a submarine. When the animal dies, its internal shell floats to the surface and is eventually driven ashore, where it may be pecked by shore birds if not collected by a budgie fancier. Caged birds find it a useful source of lime and calcium, and its abrasive quality helps them to maintain beak condition. If you give one to your budgie, first boil it well and dry it thoroughly.

The grape-like egg mass of the cuttlefish, attached to seaweed.

As molluscs, cuttlefish have an internal shell – a buoyancy device – which is often found cast ashore on the beach.

In life, the animal swims in inshore waters, hunting shrimps.

Dead birds are common objects on the strandlines, and it is always worth checking to see if they have numbered rings on their legs. In the case of racing pigeons, these should be sent, with details of place and date of recovery, to the Pigeon Racing Association, The Reddings, Cheltenham, Gloucestershire GL5 1 6RN. For all other birds, no matter what address is given on the ring, the address is the British Trust for Ornithology, Beech Grove, Tring, Hertfordshire. Do not forget to include (as well as your own address) details of recovery date, species of bird (if known) and location. In due course the organisation concerned will send you the ringing history of the bird, and you will have the satisfaction of knowing that you have added another piece to the jigsaw of information about bird life and movement.

It is possible that you might find a dead seal on the beach. In this case check the tail flippers for tags, which bear a serial number which you should send to the London Zoo at Regent's Park, which acts as a clearing house for this information. Again, send details of date, species and location, with any other information which might be helpful, and you will hear something of the history of your seal. Live seals are seldom discovered on the sort of beaches you might be walking, although occasionally, especially after the storms of early winter, a young pup might come ashore in an unsuitable place for a rest. Nine times out of ten these young seals simply want some peace and quiet, and unless they are clearly in distress, or emaciated, it is best to leave them alone, rather than trying to 'rescue' them. Most especially there is no sense in trying to get them back into the sea again. They are not fish, and choose to spend most of their time out of the water.

Whales are air-breathing mammals, too, like the seals, but in their case they are truly marine, and if you find one on the beach it is either dead or in serious trouble. On occasion they may be stranded on beaches in quite large numbers. This usually happens in the case of species which live in sociable schools, so that if a disaster happens to one it happens to the lot. There is no clear explanation for these strandings; possibly the reason is nothing more complicated than that the whales have found themselves trapped in shallow water on a falling tide. The smaller species, like dolphins, will survive for many hours, but their schooling instinct is so strong that even if some individuals are man-handled back into deep water they drive themselves back to join their mates. The larger species inevitably die when out of the water, because their sheer weight

– without the support of the surrounding water – bears down on their lungs and makes it impossible for them to breathe.

Pilot whales are sometimes stranded in large numbers, while killers and other solitary species tend to get into trouble all by themselves. Classified by the law, along with sturgeon, as 'Royal Fish', all whales caught or stranded in British waters attract a tithe rendered to the Crown in return for its protection of the coastal community from pirates and invaders. In reality they offer more of a problem than a welcome gift, and disposal of the carcass is a delicate problem for the authorities. All whale strandings should be reported to the local Coastguard, who completes a form which is sent to the British Museum (Natural History) in London. Until fairly recently it was very difficult to learn anything about the lives of sea-going mammals and much information was gleaned from the examination of corpses. Nowadays, with so many whales in captivity in large aquaria, the need is perhaps not quite so pressing.

Other animals, not so spectacular in size, but of absorbing interest, also find themselves cast ashore to meet an untimely end. The agent of their downfall is the ocean current which has carried them off course and far from home. The mighty trade winds of the equatorial region drive immense bodies of water westwards. These then swing north, travelling up the Caribbean and the east coast of the United States as the Gulf Stream and then east across the Atlantic as the North Atlantic Current. The water then flows south down the African coast and forms a surface current which circles the north Atlantic in a clockwise direction, centred on the more-or-less permanent high pressure system of the Azores. The strongest flow is in the Gulf Stream region, where it has been recorded as 218 kilometres during one day.

Much of our knowledge of surface currents comes from many years of research using drift bottles and envelopes, somewhat more serious versions of the holidaymakers' 'bottle message'. Bottle messages have a long and sometimes hilarious history, and there is plenty of evidence that they have saved lives in the past, so keep a sharp eye open! The standard time for bottle-post from New York to the coast of Europe is 550 days.

Tree-trunks and wood of all kinds are regularly carried along in the ocean currents, to be deposited far from home by the vagaries of wind and local currents. Large rocks have been rafted thousands of miles in this way, to puzzle the geologists. Rafts of matted vegetation, carrying animal passengers, have

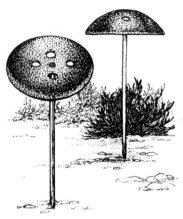

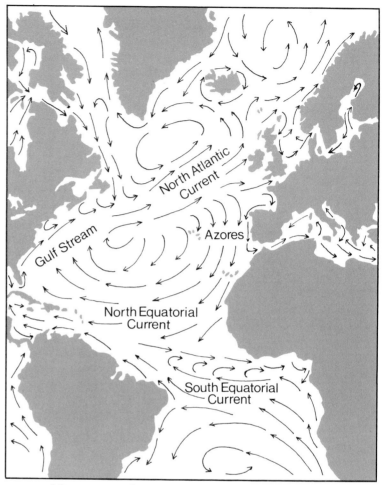

Top left Surface drift envelope.
Above Woodhead sea-bed drifters.
Above right Chart showing surface
current circulation in the North
Atlantic. Tropical beans
unfortunate enough to fall into the
Caribbean sea may find themselves
cast ashore in Western Europe. (The
chart is based on BA Chart No 5310
with the sanction of the Controller,
HM Stationery Office and of the
Hydrographer of the Navy.)

emerged from tropical estuaries to be carried out to sea. Once a
young negro was discovered, tens of miles from the mouth of
the Congo river, sitting forlornly on a floating island. Some of
these 'islands' are large enough to be a danger to shipping and
have been the subject of Notices to Mariners. Stranded trees
may even be traced back to their home valleys by a study of
their ring characteristics.

Drift wood is worthy of close inspection. There is always the
chance of a nice piece of oak for the workshop, though softwood
is more likely. Pit props are sometimes thrown ashore, and if
they have been at sea for some time they may be riddled with
the tunnellings of the shipworm. Although the exterior of the
timber may only appear to have a few small needle-holes in it,
the log will split like matchwood and the interior will reveal

an astonishing maze of chambers. In spite of its name, the shipworm is a mollusc, with two wood-boring valves at the end of its worm-shaped body. It starts life in the plankton, but on finding a sympathetic wood surface, it settles and bores a small hole to gain the safety of concealment. Once inside, it proceeds to bore and to grow (feeding on the cellulose in the wood) cutting and burrowing with a twisting movement of the shell, while the tiny entrance hole remains at its original size, closed with the calcareous 'pallet' at the animal's rear end. One of the tropical species may grow to a metre and a half in length, and the damage it may do to ships' planking or harbour installations is only too easily imagined. If you do get a chance to examine a piece of wood infested with shipworm, look for the little shell-valves and for the door-closing pallets. And notice the way that the burrowings, however random they may appear at first sight, manage to avoid disturbing the privacy of their neighbours.

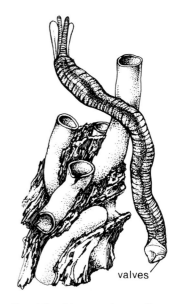

Above The shipworm is a mollusc with powerful boring valves.
Below The crustacean gribble.

Driftwood may be nibbled by the gribble, a voracious crustacean which bores and tunnels on the surface of the timber. Or it may have been a floating base for stalked barnacles, crustaceans which do no damage to the timber (though if it is part of a ship they will affect its hydrodynamic flow, and therefore its speed), but simply attach themselves to it by means of cement glands. Like the more conventional acorn barnacles ashore, the goose barnacle opens protective plates to reveal feathery cirri which filter food from the passing plankton. Originating from warmer parts of the Atlantic, these beautiful creatures are usually destined to die on our beaches, but you might find some, attached to a small piece of wood or even a bottle, which might respond, at least temporarily, to immersion in a tank of sea water. If you are lucky, they will emerge in all their feathery glory, to feed.

It was because of their feathery appearance, and the curiously beak-shaped protective plates on the neck-like stalks, that goose barnacles got their name. For many hundreds of years it was popularly believed that these barnacles were the juvenile form of the barnacle goose, and it is not at all difficult to sympathise with the misunderstanding. Often enough the barnacles are washed ashore attached to floating tree branches. So the myth took shape: 'Certain of their trees bear fruit which, decaying within, produces a worm which, as it subsequently develops, becomes hairy and feathered, and, provided with wings, flies like a bird.'

Top Thirteenth-century manuscript illustration of the barnacle goose myth – the geese hatching from a tree.
Above In reality, the goose-barnacles are stalked crustaceans which attach themselves to a convenient floating base.

Doubtless the educated mediaeval mind was well aware of the faults in this argument, but there was a powerful incentive to allow it to prevail. With such a clearly maritime origin, the barnacle goose could comfortably be classified as a fish, and as such its meat could be eaten on Fridays and feast days. It was not till 1187 that Gerald the Welshman reproved the laxity of Irish priests, and soon afterwards Innocent III forbade the practice by decree. It was the middle of the seventeenth century before a Jesuit had the temerity to declare that, though no one knew where the goose was born (in fact in Greenland, Spitzbergen and Novya Zemlya), it nevertheless was hatched from an egg, incubated like any other goose. For all that, the earlier myth was happily kept in circulation for the convenience of gourmet clerics.

Jellyfish may be stranded on the shore, and some of them may have started life thousands of miles away in the tropics. The Portuguese man-o'-war justifies its aggressive name with the power to give a nasty sting, should you be unfortunate enough to tangle with it. It may be a comfort to know that it is rarely fatal. A sub-tropical species, it sometimes strays into the Gulf Stream to find itself carried helplessly across the Atlantic to be thrown on our shores in large numbers. At first sight the bladder looks like some crude toy balloon. It is an inflated float, shimmering pale blues and pinks, up to fifteen centimetres long and with a crenellated crest looking in shape something like a crimped Cornish Pasty. Below the float hangs a complicated and tightly packed mass of polyps, for this jellyfish is a colonial species, with long tentacles bearing the stinging cells. The tentacles may be anything up to two metres long, and they can stun a fish as big as a mackerel. So, if your beach-stranded bladder comes complete with tentacles, give it a wide berth.

The Portuguese man-o'-war lives its whole life at the surface, drifting in currents, but also much influenced by the wind. The same is true of Jack-Sail-by-the-Wind, another jellyfish of warm seas, but in this case the animal is even more influenced by the wind since it has a ridge-shaped 'sail' stretched across its upper surface. Presented across the wind, the sail drives the animal slowly through the surface plankton, providing it with a choice of prey. In the face of persistent south-westerly winds, they may be blown ashore on the Atlantic coast, and the sail may last a while to puzzle beachcombers.

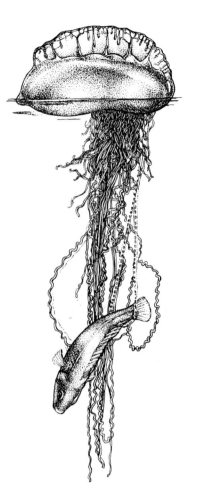

The same winds and currents which cast these tropical jellyfish ashore may also bring evidence of an ocean-going snail which preys on them, or rather on their juvenile stages. The violet sea snail lives its whole life at the surface of the sea, held there by a raft of mucus bubbles. Like the shore-living whelks, it is carnivorous, but unlike them it is not an active hunter. Instead it anaesthetises plankton prey which come into contact with it by chance, then devours them. The shell is often cast up on the strandline, but it is of a delicate nature and you will be lucky to find a perfect specimen. It is worth seeing one in a shell museum just for the pleasure of its brilliant colour.

Since the Gulf Stream passes the coast of Central America and runs amongst the sub-tropical islands of the Caribbean, it inevitably carries away seeds which find their way into the sea by way of waves, or, perhaps, birds. Doubtless the vast majority are eaten by fish as they drift along, but some survive into temperate latitudes and find their way to north-west Europe. Two beans have been recorded often enough for it to be worth keeping them in mind. *Mucuna urens* comes from the tropical mainland of central America. It is dark purple-brown and disc-shaped, with a black rim bordered creamy brown. *Entada gigas* comes from the West Indies, and is broad-bean shaped, though up to five centimetres long. It has a uniform colour, with a hard shiny skin. John Barrett, the Pembrokeshire naturalist, says that this bean is sometimes used as a teething ring for the babies

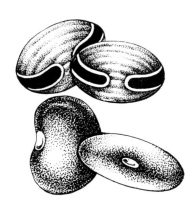

Tropical beans. *Mucuna urens* (top) and *Entada gigas*.

of fond Welsh parents. On the western coast of Ireland and in the western isles of Scotland these beans used to be known as 'Marybeans', after the Virgin Mary, because they were thought to bring the owner good fortune. Midwives gave them to women in labour, both as a lucky charm and as a distraction, rather like worry beads.

Dr Charles Nelson, National Botanic Gardens, Glasnevin, Dublin 9, is collecting information on these vegetable immigrants and where they land, so he would be delighted if you send him any strange seeds or beans you find washed up on the beach. He needs to see the bean itself because some species are very hard to identify from description alone. He would like to know where and when you found it, and also your name and address so that he can return your lucky charm.

Several species of turtle, which ought by rights to be confined to the tropical regions, find themselves in British waters, having strayed off-course during their seasonal migrations from breeding beaches to feeding grounds. Once carried off, and current-borne to our temperate zone, they have effectively committed suicide, for they cannot live long in our waters. If you do find one, it is important to inform the nearest Receiver of Wreck (at the local Custom House) or the Coast-guard, or the Natural History Museum. It is even possible that your turtle will carry a tag on the hind border of one of its front flippers, so that in due course you will learn something of its history.

One of the main pleasures of strandline walking is the anticipation of such discoveries. Truly there is no knowing what you might find amongst the random collection of specimens. Random it might appear at first glance, but apart from the gratuitous junk thrown by careless people, all the items have a past history which relates them either to the nearby shore and sea, or to far-off places by way of the mighty ocean currents.

Cliffs and caves

Beachcombers may plod along the sandy foreshore, but for distant horizons, and maybe a glimpse of some oceanic wanderer like a whale, there is nothing to beat the vantage point provided by a high cliff. When it stands squarely in the face of Atlantic storms, a cliff may be a raw and difficult habitat to colonise, but the plants and animals which live there will be correspondingly tough. Vertical cliff-faces, devoid of cracks and crevices, or cliffs formed of material so soft that it is continually weathering away, may be lifeless, but when wind, sea and weathering produce cracks and crannies, caves and ledges, then inevitably some hardy specimens take advantage of them.

The upper parts of high cliffs are usually colonised by land plants, which will use any scrap of shelter to establish themselves and will change their form if necessary to suit the local conditions, but in the lower zones, where the ability to tolerate salt spray is an environmental necessity, the maritime species come into their own. Delicate thrift and sea campion may clothe the steepest slopes and reach down nearly into the sea, and, given a measure of shelter, there may be a growth of greenery on the lower slopes which resembles a wild vegetable allotment.

Most cliff plants start life in a crevice in the rock. A crevice fills up only slowly, mostly with falls of soil from above, but also with odds and ends of soil, droppings and dead remains brought in by insects and birds. When a seed arrives, usually bird-borne, it is a toss-up whether there will be enough soil in the crevice to support life and even if the seed succeeds in germinating, it may well be dried out or uprooted by the wind. If the little plant does manage to survive these hazards, its very presence, acting as a wind-break, helps to trap more soil-building detritus. As it grows, its roots will dig deep to gain access to water, roots which are also woody and fibrous to act as an anchor against winter gales. Only the hardier plant species can survive in these harsh conditions and they tend to be perennials, wind and salt-hardened by an environment which favours maturity and discourages brash youth.

Many important cultivated plants have their origins on the coast. The sea-beet, which grows freely on shingle and on the strandline, also finds a home on cliffs, particularly on areas of disturbed ground, for instance a cliff-fall, and especially if there are bird droppings to nurture it. A coarse perennial with fleshy roots, it straggles over the ground producing a profusion of leaves. The younger leaves taste excellent prepared in the same

Sea-beet, a tough perennial which grows well on sand and shingle as well as on sea cliffs.

way as spinach, and indeed our garden spinach is a cultivated form of sea-beet. Mangold-wurzels, sugar-beet and beetroot are also close relatives. Our much-loved cabbage is a direct descendant of the wild cabbage, which is a common cliff plant with pale yellow flowers and luxuriant large blue-green leaves. Another cliff plant which has culinary value is rock samphire, whose aromatic and fleshy young leaves may be boiled as a pot herb or pickled for the benefit of its hot and spicy taste. Collected in great quantities years ago, and sold in the streets of London as 'crest marine', it was known as a valuable source of iodine, as an aid to indigestion and as a cure for scurvy.

Rock samphire, a maritime plant confined to sea cliffs, quay walls and embankments.

In the south-west there is one plant which has reversed the usual pattern by colonising cliffs after escaping from private gardens. The hottentot's fig, or mesembryanthemum, an exotic plant originating from South Africa, has established itself as a very common cliff species, festooning ledges and eclipsing almost any other plant which gets in the way. With large fleshy leaves and bright yellow flowers, it can transform the barren granite cliffs into lush tropical hanging gardens. In the Isles of Scilly it has had a marked effect on the landscape, carried to every corner by enthusiastic gardeners and also by gulls which make use of the plant for nest material.

Cliff plants are perhaps best seen by way of some sturdy climbing from the beach. Cliff birds are often best seen from the top-most point against a background of heaving sea. While the gulls are haunting the rubbish tips and begging for handouts on the promenade, the true sea-going birds may show themselves, in passing, to the patient cliff-top watcher. Choose a place

Fulmar in flight.

where the coast points a finger well out into the sea – a promontory, or perhaps the furthermost horn of a bay. The best seawatching places are those where passage birds are 'turning a corner' from one patch of sea to another, and where they are closest to land. From a good vantage point you may see distant gannets, whiter-than-white, or large parties of auks or shearwaters on migration. Although you will be lucky to see an albatross, very much a chance visitor, there is a strong likelihood of seeing a close relative – the fulmar – almost anywhere round the coast of Britain. Sit patiently at the top of a rugged cliff, and sooner or later a bold gull-like bird will soar around the corner, pass close to you with a direct stare, then glide away, perhaps to reappear a short while later to repeat the performance. The more you see of it, the clearer it becomes that it is not a gull at all. The soaring flight, the thick-necked, rather stocky appearance, and the narrow, stiffly outstretched wings, reveal the bird as a petrel, not to be written off as a 'seagull'.

Fulmars have been well established in this country for many centuries, but until relatively recently they were confined to remote islands like Foula in the Shetlands and the Hebridean St. Kilda. Over the last two hundred years, however, they have expanded their range in the most astonishing demonstration of ornithological colonisation. Nowadays, although their presence is weakest in the south-east, they nest on almost any suitable cliff in the British Isles. A bare, wind-blown ledge serves their purpose for breeding, and the single white egg is incubated without the benefit of any warmly-lined nest cup. There is no attempt at nest concealment, since the fulmar chick, which spends a good deal of time alone, has an effective and disconcerting method of discouraging intruders. Faced with an unwelcome visitor, the young bird spouts a stinking jet of fish oil through its beak, reaching a surprising distance and with surprising accuracy.

Fulmars are doing well, but not for the same reasons as gulls. They do not resort to sewage farms and fish quays; instead they benefit greatly from man's activities far out at sea. Although the precise reasons for the success of the fulmar are not universally agreed, it seems likely that the species has gained advantage from the formidable growth first in whaling and then in trawling. These industries involve the processing of fish at sea, with a consequent bonanza of offal for the scavengers. The significant warming of the north Atlantic towards the latter part of the last century may also be a factor in

Fulmar chicks repel intruders with a jet of fish-oil.

Pilot whales.

their population increase. Whatever the reason, our coasts are now much enriched by the pleasurable sight of fulmars soaring and wheeling.

Like that of the fulmar, the raven's nest is fairly easy to see, but it is usually cleverly placed and difficult to reach. Ravens choose a fair-sized ledge, usually protected by an overhanging boulder or rock-face, on which to build their nest, and, once having chosen a site, they tend to occupy it for life, although they may chop and change between two or three places not far apart. The nest itself is a massive structure, much improved as the years go by, until it becomes something of a monument. The foundations are of large dry sticks, woven together with deceptive skill to form a solid plinth. This framework is consolidated with clods of grass and soil, and the topmost sanctum is a generous cup-shape made of grasses and moss, lined with sheep's wool and rabbit fur.

The ravens, which are typical birds of the wild coast, may be seen at any time of the year. Outside the breeding season they may roost sociably on the cliffs in quite large numbers, and forage in flocks for carrion. Restless birds, they seem always to be on the move, perching first on this craggy outcrop then on that, then taking off to display an absolute mastery of the coastal air currents. Superb fliers, they soar or perform acrobatics with equal ease. Squabbling amongst themselves or mobbing an inoffensive buzzard, they are always a joy to watch. The largest of the British crows, they usually announce their presence with a deep-voiced cronking, but apart from their size, you can distinguish them by the stout black bill and the wedge-shaped tail.

A considerably less common call is the breathy, musical 'chow' of the chough. Like the raven, it is very much a crow of the wild coast, but unlike the raven its numbers have seriously declined for reasons which are not clear, although a continuous run of hard winters last century may be responsible. Unlike the other crows, this red-billed bird, the size of a jackdaw, is a choosy eater; but since it does not suffer from unreasonable competition for food it hardly seems likely that this accounts for its scarcity. Whatever the reason, choughs are now confined to the wilder coasts of the Inner Hebrides, the Isle of Man, Ireland and Wales. In the past they suffered a great deal from the activities of rabbit-catchers, whose cliff-top gin traps were unable to differentiate between the desired mammal and the non-marketable bird. On the other hand the activities of rabbits which, along with sheep, close-cropped the turf to make foraging easier for the choughs, were to its advantage. The long down-curved bill of the chough serves it well in its exploration of the grassy banks, probing for ants in their underground galleries and digging out larvae of all sorts.

In the air, choughs seem to enjoy a party. Swooping and diving, they indulge in aerial evolutions, high over the cliff face, then slide down to the very surface of the sea to fly over it with graceful ease and buoyancy. Even out of the breeding season they tend to go about in pairs. They nest in deep crevices in the cliff, very often in sea caves, high up in the roof where they are most difficult to see. In late April they build a bulky workmanlike structure of sticks, stalks and dead plants like bracken, lined with a nest-cup of wool and hair. Since they are such a decorative part of the wild coast, it is greatly to be hoped that they can overcome their problems and increase to colonise their old stamping grounds, like the coast of Cornwall. At the moment they seem to be holding their own, and presumably the shortage of peregrines is in their favour, since peregrines are their main predator.

Even the most enthusiastic chough-lover, though, must surely wish the peregrine well. Although this magnificent bird has always faced a certain amount of persecution by falconers, who prize it highly, its numbers remained stable for many hundreds of years until it was shot in wartime in order to make life easier for homing pigeons. The population, duly rising in peacetime in response to the cessation of hostilities, was then dealt a resounding blow in the late 1950s with the introduction of organo-chlorine pesticides in the agricultural industry.

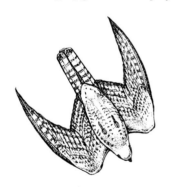

The peregrine falcon dives at a speed of up to 200 mph when attacking a pigeon or other prey.

Feeding mainly on pigeons which were eating treated grain, the peregrines accumulated the poisons in their own systems at second hand, with disastrous results to their fertility and their own lives. The partial ban on toxic farm chemicals has had a marked effect and the population of peregrines is at present slowly recovering, though hampered by the persistent efforts of egg thieves and those who misguidedly seek to become falconers without sufficient knowledge of this activity.

In the breeding season peregrines are typically falcons of the sea cliffs, nesting on ledges or in holes, at sites which may have been continuously occupied right back to mediaeval times. Perching on a rocky pinnacle, with head sunk menacingly between its shoulders, the peregrine is king of the cliffs. Fast flying machines, with pointed wings and a tapering tail, they dash about the cliff faces, keeping a weather eye open for food. Although it is true they will take a rabbit on occasion, their primary prey is seabirds and pigeons. Once decided upon, the prey, itself on the wing, is taken in flight, the peregrine swooping down with folded wings at great speed, perhaps as much as 200 miles an hour, and breaking the neck of the prey. Then, taking the carcass back to its rocky pinnacle, it plucks at it at leisure.

While the homing pigeon, crossing the coast on racing passage back to an inland loft, is certainly in danger from peregrines, in historical times the falcon would traditionally have preyed on the more purely coastal wild rock dove, as well as stock doves visiting cliff tops to forage. Nowadays the rock dove is, sadly, a decreasing species, surviving only on remote coasts and islands in Scotland and Ireland. Rock doves are perfectly at home in these wild places, and their swift and daring flight has something of the verve of the peregrine about it, though it may not be as fast as the falcon. Striking birds, rock doves have the two distinct black wing bars and whitish rump which are so often seen on the common street pigeons which live so comfortably in our cities. The connection between the two is very close and is intimately bound up with man's progress in agriculture.

Many hundreds of years ago, preserving enough food to get through the winter was much more of a problem than it is now. Few farmers could store enough hay to maintain more than a small breeding nucleus of cattle, sheep and pigs, and refrigeration was the prerogative of the very few who could afford an ice house. For most people, salted meat was the rule

Rock doves are very rare nowadays, but feral pigeons, their direct descendants, often take their place.

and fresh meat the rare exception. Rock doves, which could almost have been designed for domestication, provided the answer. Placid, with undemanding breeding requirements, their strong suit was a natural inclination to produce fat young (or squabs) at all seasons of the year, because of their ability to rear their young on pigeon 'milk'. With careful management, they could be used to provide fresh meat until the spring and summer came again. Rock doves breed in caves, and it was very soon realised that by providing extra ledges, more nests (and thus more squabs) would be produced. Before long, it was also realised that it would save a lot of trouble if the birds were brought to artificial caves, in order to spread the delights of pigeon pie to those whose residences were far from the roar of the sea. Thus dovecotes became established, and highly successful they were, providing fresh winter meat through the centuries, till eighteenth-century man discovered the potential of root crops and so cracked the problem of feeding domestic animals through the year.

Today these old pigeon houses stand idle, but the descendants of their occupants are still going strong, as street pigeons and homers. Not infrequently racing pigeons drop out of the race and retire to live on the coast. The result is that though pure rock doves may be confined to the far north and west, these impure pigeons whose remote ancestors lived on the

coasts of Britain now carry on the tradition. Feral pigeons are very common all round our coastline, living as their ancestors did, breeding in caves and foraging for seeds on the cliff tops. Though the first generation of cliff colonists may wear a racing ring, their progeny do not, and the cliffs and bays echo to the whir and clap of the wings of flocks of pigeons which are as wild as anyone might reasonably wish. Until the peregrine population is back to normal again, they are likely to flourish without check.

Apart from the rare choughs and the common pigeons, the other noteworthy inhabitant of sea caves is the grey seal. Choosing the remotest and most isolated breeding sites on islands and storm-wracked sections of the mainland, the superb grey seal is an animal totally at home in these places of fierce currents and white-water overfalls. Much persecuted in the past, seals now enjoy a certain measure of legal protection and a full measure of popular sympathy, though there is a running battle between them and the commercial fishermen, who have the usual fisherman's objection to anything which competes for their prey.

In Britain we are privileged to play host to about half the world population of grey seals, which are rare in world terms, so it behoves us to take good care of them. While it is perfectly true that grey seals have increased their numbers spectacularly since protection began, the quantity of fish they take is insignificant, compared with the annual catch of the fishing industry. It is to be hoped that long-term management plans for control of seal populations will take the welfare of the seals as their main consideration, leaving fishermen to continue enjoying the lion's share of the fish stocks.

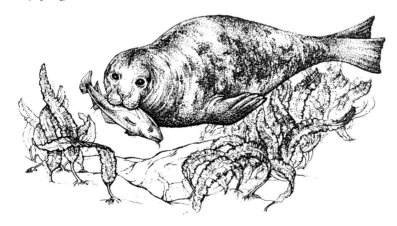

Grey seals are sociable animals, gathering close together in large numbers sometimes several hundreds at a time, for assemblies before and after the breeding season at the end of the year. On the breeding beaches, however, they tend to keep a certain distance from their fellows, and the bull seals do not come ashore at all. Choosing the remotest beach or inaccessible cave, the cow seal hauls herself up, often above high water mark, to drop her pup. It is important that even at high water of spring tides there is a strand of dry beach for the pup to rest on.

On remote beaches, grey seals may form assemblies of several hundred individuals at a time.

If the place is well chosen and undisturbed, the new-born animal may lie still, almost motionless except at feeding time, for the whole first month of its life. Often enough, though, it will go down to the water and swim about a while and then join its mother to suckle contentedly from the breast as she lies at the tide's edge.

The new-born grey seal pup has a yellowish-white coat, which turns white after a day or two.

Page 153 Grey seal pup.
A 'moulter', nearly ready to go
to sea.

Though the pup's coat is yellowish-cream at birth, the hair soon becomes white, and after a couple of weeks of rich feeding its body assumes the shape of a barrel and it begins to moult into its sea-going coat. As the grey pelage begins to appear at the head, muzzle and flippers, discarded white hairs mount up on the pebbles around the recumbent body. From a birth weight of perhaps fifteen kilogrammes, the healthy animal will have grown to about fifty kilogrammes a month later when, bloated with blubber, it is abandoned by its mother and, hungry, must find its own way to sea and learn to fish. In its first year of life it will travel, perhaps many hundreds of miles – a Welsh pup may visit France, and a Scottish or Northumberland pup may visit Norway – but in due course, if all goes well, it will return to the home beach or cave, and probably spend the rest of its life enjoying the wild seashore.

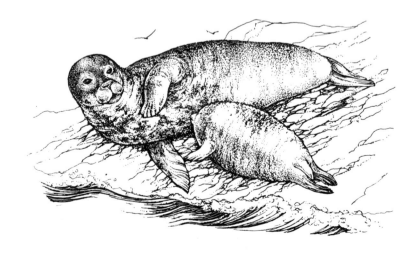

Above Thrift, or sea-pink.
Right The bright yellow flowers of
wild cabbage add another splash of
colour to the summer cliffs.
Page 155 Peregrine falcon,
undisputed king of the cliffs.

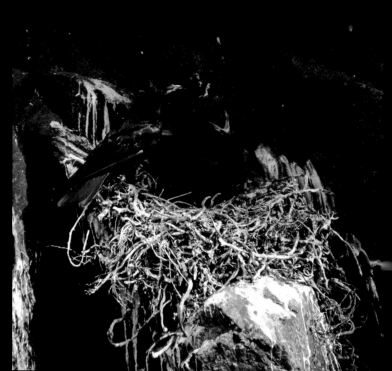

Above Choughs, with their curved red bill, are rare birds nowadays.
Above right Ravens are typically birds of the wildest exposed coast. The bulky nest may have been used and improved over many years.
Right Though pure-bred rock-doves may be rare, drop-out racing pigeons frequently breed successfully at the coast, finding their food on cliff-top and beach.

Boots, books and binoculars

One of the pleasures of coastal outings is the freedom from restraint. No one expects you to wear a tie or neatly pressed trousers when you are tramping the beaches. Yet the animals which live on the coast are specially equipped for living on the seashore and it makes sense for us, too, to bear some of the problems in mind, and to consider our own equipment very carefully.

If your object is simply to enjoy an easy day, then you will only want to carry an anorak of some kind in case the weather turns against you, but if you are likely to be collecting specimens then it makes sense to carry a shoulder bag or small rucksack. Some people take a net with them and we find it useful to take a transparent plastic sandwich box with us too. This acts as a portable aquarium, enabling you to observe animals in their natural watery environment. When all is said and done, however, there is no doubt that the less gear you carry, the more enjoyable is the day. It is very easy to add a camera and books to the load, which may seem light as you set off, but will become a wearisome burden before the sun sets!

It can on occasion be very difficult to decide what to wear on your feet. Although there is great pleasure in walking the sandflats, and even rocky ledges, in bare feet, it has to be said that there are dangers. Quite apart from broken glass and tin cans, there is the possibility of treading on the poisonous spines of a weever fish, although this is only a real danger when paddling at low water spring tides. Hilary wears flipflop shoes in this situation, but I find they trip me up only too easily, and prefer well-worn plimsolls of a vintage which has worn convenient drain-holes in them. These holes not only let the sea water run out, but also ventilate the toes in a most satisfactory manner! Gumboots are useful in winter, because they allow you to wear a pair of warm socks and (provided you are careful the sea does not slop over the top of them) to keep dry feet, but they have disadvantages. If you are going to do a lot of walking in them they tend to be tiring, but more serious is their lack of grip on the slippery seaweed surfaces of rocky ledges. If you must wear gumboots, then choose the sort made specially for yachtsmen, with flexible soles designed for gripping a heaving deck. However, be warned that in the rough conditions of the shore they have a short, and expensive, life.

Stout boots as used by walkers and climbers have no place in the seashore explorer's kit. Quite apart from the lengthy and tiresome performance of getting them on and off whenever you want to paddle in even a few inches of water, they rapidly fill with sand, which soon grates and produces blisters. The tattiest and simplest canvas-type shoes are probably the best.

Perhaps surprisingly, ordnance survey maps rarely find a place in our shore-going day bags. Almost always the actual distance covered is going to be small, so it makes more sense to have a good look at the 1:25 000 map before you set out, so that you do not have to risk getting it baptised with sea water. One of the ever-present problems is that sand and sea water have an uncanny knack of finding their way into everything you carry, and this makes life particularly difficult if you want to carry cameras. It is really vital to protect your photographic gear from drops of salt water, let alone a soaking, because sea water has quite severe corrosive properties. Our own answer to the problem is to carry optical gear in strong plastic bags, often double-wrapped inside the sort of stout plastic carrier bags that you get from supermarkets and the like. If you are carrying a rucksack of some kind, it makes good sense to throw in a few plastic bags. They weigh practically nothing and are most useful for any number of things, from keeping specimens tidy to keeping your wet bathing trunks away from your sandwiches.

Unless you are a birdwatcher, it may be as well to leave your binoculars at home. Carried round your neck they detract from the sense of freedom on the beach, and carried in your bag they are never ready when you need them most. On the other hand, if you do not have your binoculars with you, then that is bound to be the day when a school of whales blows by, or when the water's edge is alive with waders. For birdwatchers, binoculars are practically a necessity. Most birds protect themselves from their enemies by evasion and will not let you come near, no matter how patient you are. The binoculars, although they present you with a narrower field of view, bring the birds closer to you in a way that the birds themselves would never permit.

Many people find difficulty in choosing a pair of binoculars, so it may be useful to outline some of the considerations. All binoculars are described in terms of their magnification and the size of the objective lens. Thus 8 × 30 glasses magnify the image eight times (that is an object 800 metres away will appear to be 100 metres away) and have an aperture diameter of 30mm. This last measurement gives an indication of the brightness of the perceived picture, so that an aperture diameter of 25mm will give an appreciably duller picture than one of 40mm. At this point it may seem that, considerations of money apart, the glasses which give the highest possible magnification, coupled with the largest possible aperture diameter, are inevitably the best buy. This is not the case, but unfortunately it is a common misconception which is taken advantage of by mail-order advertisers, who put great stress on high magnification when offering binoculars of doubtful, and in some cases almost non-existent, value.

There are severe problems with high magnification glasses. In order to use them satisfactorily they need to be securely attached to an anchorage such as a tripod. They may be heavy, in which case the tripod needs to be heavy in turn. Any glasses with a magnification greater than $12 \times$ will almost certainly need to be fixed to something, otherwise the image will shake so much that the benefit of the enlargement is lost. If you have a steady hold, you may be able to manage $12 \times$ glasses, but only for a short time. And on a beach there is very rarely a convenient gate or post on which to rest them. Other considerations involve the weight of the binoculars (and bear in mind that by some strange magic they get heavier as the day goes by) and the resolution of the lenses. Resolution is the technical term for the quality and excellence of the optical system, and by and large you get what you pay for.

So beware of high magnification, especially if it is coupled with an inadequate aperture diameter of the objective lens. 15×30 glasses might possibly be of some value to a desert nomad, looking at distant objects in bright light, with his recumbent camel to rest on, but they will not be much use watching waders in Britain in December.

To sum up, stick to a magnification of $8 \times$ or $9 \times$ ($10 \times$ if you have steady hands) with an aperture diameter of at least 30, preferably 40 and certainly 50 if you choose the $10 \times$. Avoid mail-order except in the case of firms advertising in journals like *British Birds* or the RSPB magazine *Birds*. Try out several pairs of binoculars before you choose. For the best possible advice, see J. Flegg's pamphlet *Binoculars, telescopes and cameras for the birdwatcher*, obtainable from the British Trust for Ornithology, Beech Grove, Tring, Herts.

Although there is a bewildering choice of binoculars from which to choose, when you are considering which books to put in your bag there is less difficulty. Since there is no way in which you can carry a complete seashore library with you, you are almost certainly going to confine your choice to a bird and/or seashore field guide. We always carry the most recent edition of *Collins field guide to the birds of Britain and Europe*. For shore plants and animals we tend to dither between a longtime favourite, *The Collins pocket guide to the sea shore*, by John Barrett and C. M. Yonge, which is available in a suitably seawater-proof binding, and *The Hamlyn guide to the seashore and shallow seas of Britain and Europe* by A. C. Campbell, which has the decided merit of a more logical layout, where the pictures are arranged on opposite pages to the relevant text. Both are admirable and practically essential tools for the coast-goer.

There are many other books which could have a treasured place in your library. Perhaps the most useful thing is for us to suggest some guidelines, but in our experience librarians in any branch of the Public Library system are willing to give advice.

*ANGEL, H. *The world of an estuary* Faber, 1974
*BARRETT, J. *Life on the sea shore* Collins, 1974
CAMPBELL, B. *Birds of coast and sea: Britain and Northern Europe* OUP, 1977
CHAPMAN, V. J. *Coastal vegetation* Pergamon Press, n.e. cased and paperback 1976
CHAPMAN, V. J. *Seaweeds and their uses* Methuen, n.e. 1970
*CRAMP, S. *The seabirds of Britain and Ireland* Collins, 1977
ELTRINGHAM, S. K. *Life in mud and sand* ULP, 1971
FISHER, J. and LOCKLEY, R. M. *Seabirds* Collins, 1954 op
FRASER, F. C. *British whales, dolphins, and porpoises* British Museum Natural History, n.e. 1976
FRIEDRICH, H. *Marine biology* Sidgwick and Jackson, 1970
GIBSON-HILL, C. A. *A guide to the birds of the coast* Constable, 1976
GREEN, J. *The biology of estuarine animals* Sidgwick and Jackson, 1968 op
*HARDY, SIR A. *The open sea* Collins, 2 Vols. n.e. 1970–71
LEWIS, J. R. *The ecology of rocky shores* EUP, 1964; Hodder, n.e. paperback 1976
*NICHOLS, D. *The Oxford book of invertebrates* OUP, 1971
*RUSSELL, F. S. and YONGE, C. M. *The seas* Warne, n.e. 1975
STEERS, J. A. *The sea coast* Collins, 1954
YONGE, C. M. and THOMPSON, T. E. *Living marine molluscs* Collins, 1976
*YONGE, C. M. *The sea shore* Collins, n.e. 1966

Strongly recommended

In drawing up this code, the Nature Conservancy Council had particularly in mind the activities of educational field courses, skin divers, sea anglers and bait diggers, but the suggestions are equally relevant for all who visit the seashore.

The Coastal Code

Our coasts are increasingly being used for education, and more and more pressure is being exerted on their plant and animal life. Unless we are careful we will destroy the very features we have come to study and enjoy. If future generations are to enjoy the richness of our shores and shallow seas, remember . . .

DON'T DISTURB
DON'T DESTROY
ACT RESPONSIBLY
FOLLOW THE COUNTRY CODE

Disturbance

Disturbance for many animals can affect their breeding cycles and feeding behaviour and in some instances even cause death.

Do not turn rocks over unnecessarily and always return them to their original position, taking care not to crush animals and plants beneath them.

When taking photographs avoid disturbing the subject and its surroundings and always leave everything as you found it. An animal exposed for a photograph is also exposed to predators.

Trampling can damage sand dunes, cliff tops and salt marshes by destroying their protective covering of plant life.

Spread the area from which you collect bait and always back fill holes you've dug.

Destruction

Demonstrate living material without removing it.
Do not mark animals without expert advice. Bad
marking can kill or expose an animal to predators.
Don't collect living plants and animals. Empty shells
make the best souvenirs. Identify plants and animals by
taking the book to the shore, not the shore to the book.
Sea urchins and sea fans take years to grow. Please leave
them alone.
Spear fishing makes fish shy of divers. Don't spearfish for
wrasse and other inshore species. Once an area is depleted
of fish it may take a long time for them to recolonise it.

Carelessness

Boat fuel will kill marine life, use it with care.
Litter is both dangerous and unsightly.
Take it home with you.
Spear fishing is dangerous near other water users.
Discarded fishing line and nets can trap and kill sea birds.
If on an educational trip make your visit instructive not
destructive; follow the Outdoor Studies Code and the code
for Geological Fieldwork.

*When recording at sites of special scientific interest or nature
reserves, send a copy of your results to the Institute of
Terrestrial Ecology, Biological Records Centre, Abbots
Ripton, Huntingdon. Also to the appropriate Regional officer
of the Nature Conservancy Council.*

The Outdoor Studies Code is
obtainable from the Resources
Committee of the Council for
Environmental Education,
9 Devereux Court, Strand WC2 3JR,
and the Code for Geological Field
Work from The Geologists'
Association, c/o Department of
Geology, University College London,
Gower Street, London WC1E 6BT.

Scientific names of species mentioned in this book

Angler fish *Lophius piscatorius*
Aster, sea *Aster tripolium*
Avocet *Avocetta recurvirostra*

Barnacle, acorn *Balanus sp.*
Barnacle, goose *Lepas anatifera*
Bass *Dicentrarchus labrax*
Bittern *Botaurus stellaris*
Bluebell *Endymion non-scriptus*
Bracken *Pteridium aquilinum*
Butterfish *Pholis gunnellus*

Campion, red *Silene dioica*
Campion, sea *Silene maritima*
Celandine, lesser *Ranunculus ficaria*
Chiton *Lepidochitona cinereus*
Chough *Pyrrhocorax pyrrhocorax*
Cockle, common *Cardium edule*
Cod *Gadus morhua*
Cord grass *Spartina townsendii*
Cormorant *Phalacrocorax carbo*
Crab, edible *Cancer pagurus*
   hermit *Eupagurus sp.*
   long-clawed porcelain
      Porcellana longicornis
   masked *Corystes cassivelaunus*
   shore *Carcinus maenas*
   spiny spider *Maia squinado*
Crawfish *Palinurus vulgaris*
Crow *Corvus corax*
Curlew *Numenius arguata*

Dogfish, greater spotted
      Scyliorhinus stellaris
   lesser spotted
      Scyliorhinus caniculus
Dolphin, bottle-nosed
      Tursiops truncatus
Dove, rock *Columba livia*
Dunlin *Calidris alpina*

Eel, common *Anguilla anguilla*
   conger *Conger conger*

Flounder *Platichthys flesus*
Fox *Vulpes vulpes*
Fulmar *Fulmarus glacialis*

Gannet *Sula bassana*
Gaper, sand *Mya arenaria*
Glasswort *Salicornia europaea*
Godwit, black-tailed *Limosa limosa*
   bar-tailed *Limosa lapponica*

Goose, barnacle *Branta leucopsis*
   brent *Branta bernicla*
Grass, lyme *Elymus arenarius*
   marram *Ammophila arenaria*
   sand couch *Agropyron junceiforme*
Gribble *Limnoria lignorum*
Guillemot *Uria aalge*
Gull, black-headed *Larus ridibundus*
   greater black-backed *Larus marinus*
   herring *Larus argentatus*
   kittiwake *Rissa tridactyla*
   lesser black-backed *Larus fuscus*
Gurnard, red *Trigla cuculus*

Haddock *Melanogrammus aeglefinus*
Harrier, marsh *Circus aeruginosus*
Hawkbit, hairy *Leontoplon hispiclus*
Heron, grey *Ardea cinerea*
Herring *Clupea harengus*

Ivy, ground *Glechoma hederacea*

Jackdaw *Corvus monedula*
Jack sail-by-the-wind *Velella velella*
John Dory *Zeus faber*

Lark, sky *Alauda arvensis*
Lavender, sea *Limonium vulgare*
Limpet, common *Patella vulgata*
Ling *Molva molva*
Lobster *Homarus vulgaris*
Lugworm *Arenicola marina*

Mackerel *Scomber scombrus*
Mallard *Anas platyrhynchos*
Mussel *Mytilus edulis*

Newt, smooth *Triturus vulgaris*

Oarweed *Laminaria digitata*
Octopus *Octopus vulgaris*
Osprey *Pandion haliaetus*
Owl, short-eared *Asio flammeus*
Oystercatcher *Haematopus astralegus*

Peregrine *Falco peregrinus*
Periwinkle, common *Littorina littorea*
   flat *Littorina littoralis*
   rough *Littorina saxatilis*
   small *Littorina neritoides*
Pipit, rock *Anthus spinoletta*

Piddock, common *Pholas dactylus*
Plaice *Pleuronectes platessa*
Plantain, buck's-horn *Plantago coronopus*
Plover, ringed *Charadrius hiaticula*
Pollack *Pollachius pollachius*
Porpoise, common *Phocaena phocaena*
Portuguese man-o-war *Physalia physalia*
Puffin *Fratercula arctica*
Purslane, sea *Halimione portucaloides*

Rabbit *Oryctolagus cuniculus*
Ragwort *Senecio jacobaea*
Razorbill *Alca torda*
Razorshell *Ensis sp.*
Raven *Corvus corax*
Ray, thornback *Raja clavata*
Redshank *Tringa totanus*
Reedling, bearded *Panurus biarnicus*

Salmon, Atlantic *Salmo salar*
Samphire, rock *Crithmum maritimum*
Sanderling *Calidris alba*
Sandpiper, purple *Calidris maritima*
Scallop, great *Pecten maximus*
  queen *Chlamys opercularis*
Scoter, common *Melanitta nigra*
Sea beet *Beta maritima*
Sea slater *Ligia oceanica*
Sea potato *Echinocardium cordatum*
Sea urchin *Echinus esculentus*
seal, common *Phoca vitulina*
  grey *Halichoerus grypus*
Sedge, sand *Carex arenaria*
Shag *Phalacrocorax aristotelis*
Shark, basking *Cetorhinus maximus*
  blue *Prionace glauca*
  porbeagle *Lamna nasus*
Shearwater, manx *Puffinus puffinus*
Shelduck *Tadorna tadorna*

Shell, peppery furrow *Scrobicularia plana*
Shipworm *Teredo sp.*
Snail, violet sea *Ianthina janthina*
Spoonbill *Platalea leucorodia*
Squid, common *Loligo forbesi*
Starfish, burrowing *Astropecten irregularis*
  common *Asterias rubens*
Swan, mute *Cygnus olor*

Teal *Anas crecca*
Tellin, Baltic *Macoma balthica*
Tern, arctic *Sterna paradisaea*
  common *Sterna hirundo*
  little *Sterna albifrons*
  sandwich *Sterna sandvicensis*
Thrift *Armeria maritima*
Toad, natterjack *Bufo calamita*
Tope *Galeorhinus galeus*
Turbot *Scophthalmus maximus*
Turnstone *Arenaria interpres*

Vole, Skomer *Clethrionomys glareolus (Skomer)*

Whale, pilot *Globicephala melaena*
Whelk, common *Buccinum undatum*
  dog *Nucella lapillus*
  netted dog *Nassarius reticulatus*
Whimbrel *Numenius phaeopus*
Wigeon *Anas penelope*
Wrack, bladder *Fucus vesiculosus*
  channelled *Pelvetia canaliculata*
  knotted *Ascophyllum nodosum*
  serrated *Fucus serratus*
  sugary *Laminaria saccharina*
  spiral *Fucus spiralis*

Index

Acknowledgements

Many people helped us with information for this book, and many helped
Ron Bloomfield and Judy Brooks in the production of the associated film series, but in
particular we should like to mention Michael Alexander, Warden of Skomer Island;
Prof. John Allen, Director of the University Marine Biological Station, Millport, Isle of
Cumbrae; Linda Blakemore, the book designer; Jim Curtis, Ministry of Agriculture,
Fisheries and Food, Fisheries Officer at Newlyn; Ted Eales of Blakeney Point Nature
Reserve; Hugh Goodson and Chris Bircham of Dart Oyster Fisheries; David Hunt,
RSPB representative for the Isles of Scilly; Les Jackman; Charles Johnson, Warden of
Holkham Nature Reserve; Chris Mead, British Trust for Ornithology; Dr Geoffrey
Potts and Dr Quentin Bone of the Marine Biological Association of the United
Kingdom; Robin and Judy Pratt of Ramsey Island; David Saunders of the West Wales
Naturalists Trust; Judy Savage, photo researcher; David Streeter of the University
of Sussex.

Acknowledgement is due to the following for permission to reproduce photographs:
AEROFILMS estuary page 91, Isle of Wight page 115; HEATHER ANGEL rocks page 9,
piddock borings page 35, heart urchin and starfish page 37, starfish and netted dog
whelks page 38, lugworm casts page 40, sand mason worms page 41, sea potato
page 42, cockle page 43, razor shell page 46, crab page 48, limpets and cowrie
page 55, beadlet anemones page 56, sea urchin page 57, hermit crab page 58,
oarweeds page 59, acorn barnacles page 65, dog whelks page 66, marram grass
page 75, Dee estuary page 89, rice grass and glasswort page 93, knots page 94,
whelk eggs page 130, strand lines page 131, goose barnacles page 138, thrift and
wild cabbage page 152, pigeon page 154; AQUILA PHOTOGRAPHICS gull page 113,
Manx Shearwater page 122; ARDEA PHOTOGRAPHICS (photo A. & E. Bomford) gannets
page 19, (photo J. L. Mason) natterjack toad page 75, (photos R. J. C. Blewitt)
razorbill page 113 and kittiwakes and guillemots page 124, (photo Richard
Vaughan) razorbills page 124; ROBERT ATKINSON seals page 150; PETER BAKER fishing
boat page 11, unloading fish page 30; BARNABY'S PICTURE LIBRARY (photo Graham
Cooper) beach page 33, (photo Betty Rawlings) surfing page 39, (photo Les Owen)
groynes page 46, (photo R. W. Kennedy) sanderling page 48, (photo T. H. Williams)
seashore page 49, (photo Hubertus Kanus) cliffs page 141, (photo J. B.) whales
page 145, (photo A. S. Blair) pigeons page 148; RODNEY BOND dolphin page 131,
worm holes page 132; BRITISH LIBRARY barnacle geese Ms. Harl. 4751 f.36 page 138;
BRITISH TRAWLERS FEDERATION (photo Peter Waugh) cod end page 29; JUDY BROOKS
Skomer page 112; CAMERA PRESS (photo Ken Lambert) beach page 6, (photo Billed)
trawler page 30; BRUCE COLEMAN LTD (photo Jane Burton) plaice page 17, rabbit
page 112, (photo Eric Crighton) pulpit rock page 51, (photo Udo Hirsch) sandwich
terns page 76, (photo D. & K. Urry) puffin page 114, (photos L. R. Dawson) ravens
and chough page 154; JOHN M. DAVIS ASSOCIATES (photo Walter Fussey & Son) trawler
page 30; ESSO netting salmon page 101; F. E. GIBSON cuttlefish page 133; from
P. H. GOSSE 'A Year at the Shore' 1865 shrimp and prawn page 53; ERIC HOSKING sea
holly page 75, shelduck page 76, oystercatcher page 79, sandwich terns page 87,
godwit page 93, peregrine falcon page 153, seal pup page 155; INSTITUTE OF
GEOLOGICAL SCIENCES Staffa page 51; LESLIE JACKMAN dunes page 71, gulls page 76;
JAN VAN DE KAM dunlin page 105; A. F. KERSTING Skomer page 112; NATURAL HISTORY
PHOTOGRAPHIC AGENCY (photo D. N. Dalton) common scoter page 19; OXFORD
SCIENTIFIC FILMS dinoflagellate page 18; PRESS ASSOCIATION collecting seaweed page
129; RADIO TIMES HULTON PICTURE LIBRARY shrimping page 53; RSPB (photo Keri
Williams) sandpiper page 69, (photos Michael W. Richards) hide page 87, heron
page 93, gannets page 124, (photo P. van Groenendael and W. Suetens) osprey page
101, (photo Dennis Green) redshanks page 105; SEA MAMMAL RESEARCH UNIT, CAMBS.
seal beach page 74, seals page 77; SEAPHOT (photo Peter Scoones) mackerel page 20,
mussel page 45, (photo Colin Doeg) shark page 23; TONY SOPER limpets page 57,
strandline page 127, pollution card page 136, seal pup page 151, seal page 156;
WEST AIR PHOTOGRAPHY Skomer page 109; D. P. WILSON plankton page 12 and 18 top,
scallops page 38, velella and violet sea snail page 132.

The photographs on the front cover and page 157 were specially taken by
Nicholas Horne.